VIETNAM STUDIES

THE WAR IN THE NORTHERN PROVINCES 1966–1968

by

Lieutenant General Willard Pearson

DEPARTMENT OF THE ARMY
WASHINGTON, D.C., 1975

Library of Congress Catalog Number: 75–23360
First Printing

For sale by the Superintendent of Documents, U.S. Government Printing Office
Washington, D.C. 20402

Foreword

The United States Army has met an unusually complex challenge in Southeast Asia. In conjunction with the other services, the Army has fought in support of a national policy of assisting an emerging nation to develop governmental processes of its own choosing, free of outside coercion. In addition to the usual problems of waging armed conflict, the assignment in Southeast Asia has required superimposing the immensely sophisticated tasks of a modern army upon an underdeveloped environment and adapting them to demands covering a wide spectrum. These involved helping to fulfill the basic needs of an agrarian population, dealing with the frustrations of antiguerrilla operations, and conducting conventional campaigns against well-trained and determined regular units.

Although this assignment has officially ended, the U.S. Army must prepare for other challenges that may lie ahead. While cognizant that history never repeats itself exactly and that no army ever profited from trying to meet a new challenge in terms of the old one, the Army nevertheless stands to benefit immensely from a study of its experience, its shortcomings no less than its achievements.

Aware that some years must elapse before the official histories will provide a detailed and objective analysis of the experience in Southeast Asia, we have sought a forum whereby some of the more salient aspects of that experience can be made available now. At the request of the Chief of Staff, a representative group of senior officers who served in important posts in Vietnam and who will carry a heavy burden of day-to-day responsibilities has prepared a series of monographs. These studies should be of great value in helping the Army develop future operational concepts while at the same time contributing to the historical record and providing the American public with an interim report on the performance of men and officers who have responded, as others have through our history, to exacting and trying demands.

All monographs in the series are based primarily on official records, with additional material from published and unpublished secondary works, from debriefing reports and interviews with key participants, and from the personal experience of the author. To facilitate security clearance, annotation and detailed bibliography have been omitted from the published version; a fully documented account with bibliography is filed with the U.S. Army Center of Military History.

The reader should be reminded that most of the writing was accomplished while the war in Vietnam was at its peak, and the monographs frequently refer to events of the past as if they were taking place in the present.

The author of this monograph, Lieutenant General Willard Pearson, played a significant role in the events he so graphically describes. During the *Tet* offensive of 1968 he organized a MACV Forward Command Post and directed its deployment to Phu Bai in the I Corps Tactical Zone. He later served as Deputy Commander and Chief of Staff of XXIV Army Corps, an enlarged and reorganized outgrowth of MACV Forward. In 1966, on an earlier tour of duty in Vietnam, General Pearson commanded the 1st Brigade of the 101st Airborne Division. Under General Pearson's command, the brigade saw action in ten different provinces and earned a Presidential Unit Citation. A veteran of World War II and the Korean conflict, General Pearson is presently Superintendent of the Valley Forge Military Academy and Jr. College, Wayne, Pennsylvania.

15 March 1974
Washington, D.C.

VERNE L. BOWERS
Major General, USA
The Adjutant General

Preface

The North Vietnamese Army units deployed just north of the demilitarized zone in 1966 posed a serious and continuing threat to the security of Quang Tri and Thua Thien, the two northernmost provinces of South Vietnam. This is an account of the North Vietnamese attempts to seize control of these two provinces and of the response of the Free World Military Assistance Forces. The period covered by this narrative is from the spring of 1966 to the spring of 1968 and is the story, primarily, of U.S. Army units.

Particular appreciation is due Major John F. Reid, Infantry, who researched and compiled the initial draft of the narrative and Specialist 7 Gary L. Neal, who was the author's stenographer during the critical months of the *Tet* offensive at Phu Bai in February and March 1968 and who four years later typed the final draft for the author at Headquarters, V Corps, Frankfurt, Germany.

Wayne, Pennsylvania   WILLARD PEARSON
15 March 1974   Lieutenant General, US Army

Contents

Illustrations

THE WAR IN
THE NORTHERN PROVINCES

CHAPTER I

Early Developments

Background

Quang Tri and Thua Thien, the northernmost provinces of the Republic of Vietnam, are more than 450 miles from Saigon, the capital. They are bordered on the north by the demilitarized zone, on the south by Quang Nam Province, on the east by the South China Sea, and on the west by the mountainous Laotian frontier.

Except for the narrow piedmont coastal plains, the terrain is dominated by hills and the Annamite Mountains. The highlands, characterized by steep slopes, sharp crests, and narrow valleys, are covered mainly by a dense broadleaf evergreen forest. Most of the peaks are from 4,000 to 7,000 feet high, but some rise above 8,000 feet. The narrow coastal plains flanking the highlands on the east are compartmented by rocky headlands and consist of belts of sand dunes and, in areas where the soil is suitable, rice fields.

From the crests that mark the drainage divide in the highlands, streams flow either east towards the South China Sea or west into Laos or Cambodia. Those flowing eastward are swift and follow short courses through deep narrow valleys over rocky bottoms until they reach the coastal plains, where they slow down and disperse over silty and sandy bottoms. The westward flowing streams follow longer traces, sometimes through deep canyons, other times through poorly drained valleys that, like the coastal plains in the east, are subject to seasonal flooding.

From a military point of view, operations were most affected by the rugged, forested mountains and hills, and the seasonally flooded lowland plains with their dense pattern of agricultural features. It was in the canopied forest, steep rugged mountains, dense undergrowth, and jungle along the demilitarized zone at the Rock Pile, Khe Sanh, and A Shau that much of the heavy fighting was to take place.

Weather played a dominant role in operations—particularly during the *Tet* offensive and subsequent operations at Khe Sanh and A Shau. The northeastern coast of South Vietnam and the adjacent Laotian panhandle are under the prevailing influence of a monsoon climate characterized by distinct wet and dry seasons.

Generally, the time of the southwest monsoon from May through September is a dry, hot, and dusty season in the mountain plateau and plains of the northeast coast. Across the mountains to the west in the Laotian panhandle, this same season brings heavy and frequent precipitation, high humidity, maximum cloudiness of the cumulus type permitting relatively good visibility and, except at the greater elevations, high temperatures. In contrast the northeast monsoon from November to mid-March carries the wet season to the coastal region of Vietnam while across the mountains in Laos the weather is hot and dry. During the wet season in the northern provinces temperatures often drop to 45 degrees, requiring issuance of warm clothing to the troops—an important logistical consideration.

Separating these major seasons are short transitional periods. From January through April the mountain plateau and northeast coast are also subject to the "crachin," a period of low cloud, fog, and drizzle or light rain which reduces ceilings and visibility. Another aspect of the weather is the combination of torrential rain and flash floods, which created flood conditions for units in base areas and on the march alike. The floods cost lives, damaged and destroyed property, and remained a contingency that commanders always had to be prepared to meet. In I Corps Tactical Zone both the northeast and the southeast monsoons exerted an influence on military operations unmatched elsewhere in Vietnam.

Transportation facilities in the region were poorly developed. Only one all-weather road, Route 9, connected the coast of Quang Tri province with the western mountains. In Thua Thien an extremely primitive road, Route 547, ran south and west from Hue into the A Shau Valley. The major north-south road was Highway 1, which ran north from the port of Da Nang in Quang Nam Province through the Hai Van Pass to Hue. From Hue the road continued north through the towns of Quang Tri and Dong Ha to Gio Linh, almost at the demilitarized zone, thence on into North Vietnam. North of the Hai Van Pass there were no all-weather ports. (Map 1)

By far the most important city in the region was Hue, the ancient imperial capital of Vietnam in Thua Thien Province about twelve kilometers from the sea. A city with a population of more than 100,000, it was the center of a serious Buddhist uprising in March of 1966.

The war in Vietnam was a fluid one with no front lines. The enemy was tough, versatile, tenacious, and cunning. He possessed strong entrenchments in the villages, mountain hideouts, and jungle redoubts. He was difficult to find and identify. At one end of the

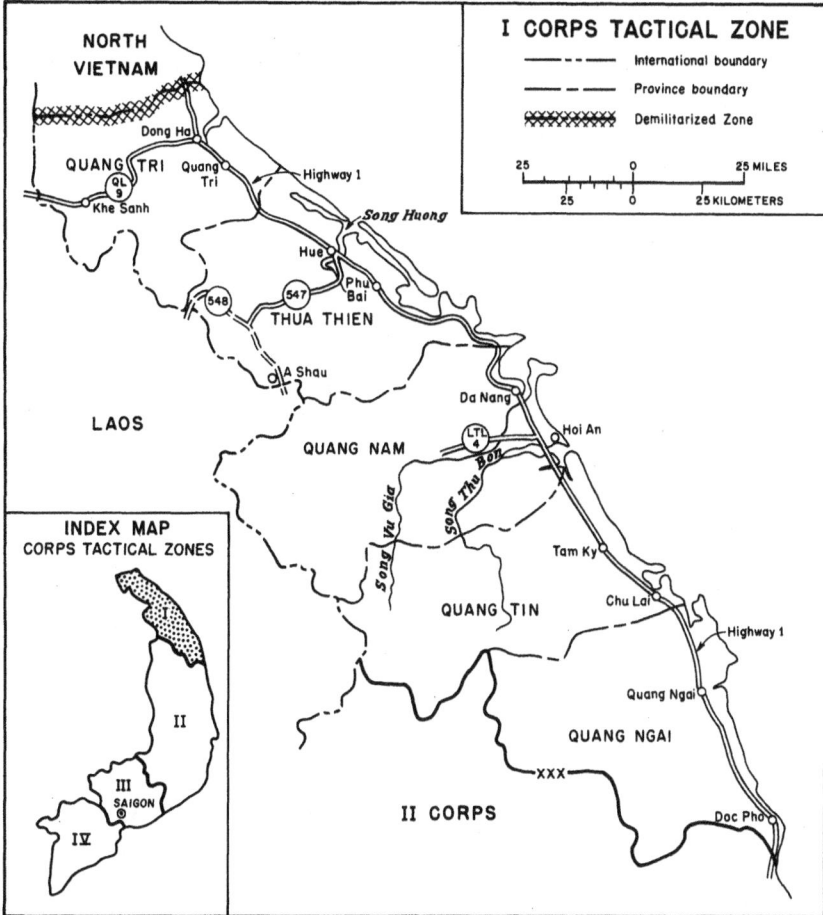

MAP 1

spectrum he merged into the civilian population as an agent or guerrilla or civil official wearing no uniform, unarmed, and supported by a military political organization. At the other end of the spectrum he was a uniformed member of the regular North Vietnamese Army. The North Vietnamese and Viet Cong fighters possessed as much courage and motivation as any foe to face the American soldier. They proved a formidable adversary.

The composition of the U.S. military forces opposing the North Vietnamese was heterogeneous. The U.S. Marine Corps units were the first committed. As the enemy threat developed, U.S. Army artillery units were deployed north to reinforce the marines. The artillery was followed by other tactical, combat support, and combat service support elements, including a chemical smoke generator company. These, like the artillery reinforcements, came under operational control of the commanding general of the III Marine Amphibious Force. The U.S. Navy provided logistical support for the marines from the sea as well as along the inland waterways. Air operations were undertaken by the Air Force, Navy, Marine Corps, and Vietnamese Air Force while the Army and Marine Corps furnished helicopter units.

It was necessary to integrate these diverse U.S. forces with the equally diverse Vietnamese forces that included the Army of Vietnam, Regional Forces, Popular Forces, Civilian Irregular Defense Group, Vietnamese Air Force, and Navy elements. All came under Vietnamese commanders responsive to headquarters in Saigon.

The demilitarized zone served as a line of demarcation between air and ground commanders. The air forces were responsible for the area north of the zone and the ground forces for the area south of it. Initially Marine gound elements had to obtain authority from the Air Force before firing counterbattery fire against North Vietnamese Army artillery just across the demilitarized zone and well within range of Marine Corps artillery. Later, responsibility for the area north of the zone was given to the Marine forces out to the range of their artillery, and thereafter, the U.S. Air Force coordinated with the ground troops prior to executing strikes in the area falling within range of the Marine artillery.

The Northern Border, 1965–1967

The first American combat forces were committed to the I Corps Tactical Zone in March of 1965 when two U.S. Marine battalions landed at Da Nang. Initially employed for the defense of the airbase at that city, the Marine battalions began limited offensive operations in April.

By the end of June 1965 the Marine strength had increased to seven battalions and was designated the III Marine Amphibious Force, under the command of Major General Lewis W. Walt, who also commanded the Third Marine Division. Operating from bases at Chu Lai, Da Nang, and Phu Bai near Hue, the Marines conducted operations against the enemy. The most successful of these, Operation STARLIGHT, resulted in the virtual destruction of two enemy battalions trapped against the South China Sea near Chu Lai.

By the spring of 1966, however, a new threat developed as the enemy began preparations for what appeared to be a major attack across the demilitarized zone. The enemy opened his offensive in March 1966 when the 95B and 101C Regiments of the North Vietnamese Army attacked a Special Forces camp located in the remote A Shau Valley in western Thua Thien province.

AERIAL VIEW OF A SHAU SPECIAL FORCES CAMP

After three days of valiant and heavy fighting in extreme weather, the Civilian Irregular Defense Group forces and a small detachment of U.S. and Vietnamese Special Forces abandoned the camp. Men of the Special Forces, Marine, Air Force, and Army helicopter units performed bravely in supporting and withdrawing these troops. Short of troops and helicopters and threatened by a major invasion along the demilitarized zone, General William C. Westmoreland, Commander, U.S. Military Assistance command, Vietnam, decided against reinforcing or reoccupying the remote camp of A Shau. Two years would pass before any Free World Forces would be able to return to this valley. After the United States abandoned the camp, North Vietnamese moved into the A Shau Valley and began to develop major logistical bases and to construct roads into Laos to tie in with the extensive network of trafficable routes leading from North Vietnam. During 1966, more than 58,000 men, the equal of five divisions, infiltrated South Vietnam. The enemy's strength throughout South Vietnam at the end of 1966 exceeded 280,000 and was augmented with an estimated 80,000 additional political cadre.

As the number of enemy personnel increased, so too did the

quality of enemy arms. A marked increase in the number of light-weight RPG2 rocket launchers which had been first employed in 1964 was noted. In attacks against the Special Forces camp at Khe Sanh and the Da Nang Airfield in January 1966, the use of 120-mm. mortars almost doubled the distance from which the enemy could conduct mortar attacks against these Free World installations. This ability sharply magnified U.S. base defense problems. Viet Cong and local guerrilla forces began to appear with the AK47, a Chinese Communist copy of the Soviet AK47 assault rifle, a highly effective automatic weapon.

U.S. commanders marked the infiltration of new enemy divisions and the stockpiling of equipment. In studying the enemy situation General Westmoreland concluded that the enemy intended to open a new front in northern I Corps to divert Free World Forces from the heavily populated region around Saigon which was the enemy's preferred objective. General Westmoreland also believed that the enemy hoped to seize and hold the northern areas as a base for a so-called liberation regime that could be parlayed into a winning "compromise" in future peace talks. The ultimate goal appeared to be the seizure of complete control of the two northern provinces. From the enemy point of view, the northern provinces of I Corps had advantageous features. Thua Thien province was in a state of critical political unrest, and the South Vietnamese government control of the province was severely challenged by dissident elements. From March until mid-summer of 1966, the government experienced a series of political crises as the Struggle Movement of militant Buddhists and students resorted to riots and civil disorders throughout the country; the situation was particularly acute in Hue and Da Nang.

The antigovernment movement was infiltrated by Communists and it appeared at the time to be taking over the northern portion of the country. In an effort to quell the trouble, the Saigon government removed the I Corps Commander, Lieutenant General Nguyen Chanh Thi, but mass protests nevertheless spread and continued until mid-summer.

Premier Nguyen Cao Ky flew to Da Nang in an attempt to end the rebellion there. In mid-April, a national political congress met in Saigon to adopt a program designed to meet the Buddhists' demands. The demonstrations soon ended, and by mid-May government troops regained control of Da Nang. Even so, the aftermath of bitterness and disaffection lingered, and the loyalty of many Vietnamese army troops in the northern region remained questionable since some had actively supported the rebel movement.

One other factor which drew the attention of the Communists

to northern I Corps was its proximity to North Vietnam and the subsequent need for shorter land routes for resupply and reinforcement.

In early 1966, the Communists transferred Quang Tri and Thua Thien provinces from their Region Five headquarters in the Central Highlands and placed them under Region Four, which included the area just north of the demilitarized zone in North Vietnam. This move was considered a possible indication that the Communists hoped to place the two provinces within North Vietnam's boundary as a bargaining point in any peace negotiations. The fact that the city of Hue is in one of these provinces was of considerable importance, and, to this day, Hue remains the traditional cultural and religious center of South Vietnam and of great psychological importance to the Vietnamese.

With North Vietnamese entering Quang Tri province from the north and west in divisional strength and with the U.S. Marines, U.S. Army, and South Vietnamese pushing north and west from the coast, a major clash seemed inevitable. The Free World Forces had watched the enemy buildup and advance closely from March through June and by mid-July were prepared to act.

Operation Hastings

The major clash between the allies and the invading North Vietnamese occurred in July 1966. For several weeks before this time Marine reconnaissance teams had been sighting groups of North Vietnamese near the village of Cam Lo in the east central part of Quang Tri Province. By early July reconnaissance teams in the Cam Lo area were almost invariably finding themselves in contact with large enemy units. Interrogation of prisoners and analyses of captured enemy documents confirmed that no fewer than 5,000 regulars of the 324B Division of the North Vietnamese Army were in South Vietnam, preparing to overrun Quang Tri Province.

To counter the coming attack General Walt, Commander of the III Marine Amphibious Force, had available only one reinforced Marine division, the Third, a Vietnamese Army division, the First, and some smaller Vietnamese Marine units. General Walt's other Marine division, the First, was fully occupied with security and pacification operations in southern I Corps.

On July 11, the Marine and South Vietnamese commanders met in Hue to plan an operation to counter the enemy threat. The direct result was Operation HASTINGS, the largest operation of the war to date and one involving more than 8,000 Marines, 3,000 South Vietnamese, and perhaps as many as 12,500 enemy troops.

The operation, under the command of Brigadier General Lo-

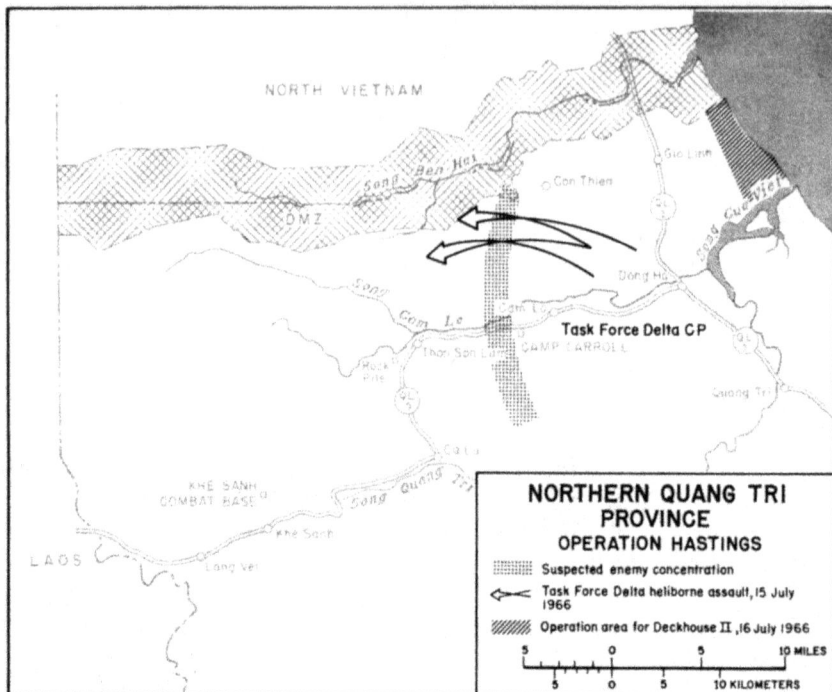

MAP 2

well E. English, United States Marine Corps, began at 0800 on July 15 when the Marines executed a heliborne assault to secure landing sites to the rear of the North Vietnamese positions. (*Map 2*) The first lift enjoyed a relatively uneventful landing, but contact became heavy as subsequent lifts touched down. Using these contacts and intelligence acquired by reconnaissance units of both the Marines and Vietnam Army, the commanders were able to position forces in areas where they could achieve excellent results. Many enemy positions were overrun and large quantities of equipment, clothing, and other supplies were captured.

The enemy initially chose to stand and fight but soon revised his thinking and attempted to evade the Marine and Vietnamese Army forces. The marines uncovered several recently abandoned company-size bivouac areas with everything intact except the weapons, indicating that a large unit was probably trying to evade the task force. A regimental- or division-size command post was discovered with supplies for 500 men in the Dong Ha Mountains. It was surmised that Operation HASTINGS had pre-empted a major enemy attack. U.S. forces, together with the Vietnamese, had joined the battle with sufficient knowledge about the enemy to hold the initiative from the first day.

175-MM. GUN

The Continuing Threat of Invasion

By the end of July the 324B Division was withdrawing across the demilitarized zone to North Vietnam. Certain elements of the division had suffered severely, but the division itself remained intact. The North Vietnamese had been forced into action before they had completed their deployment, but they retained their unity and control. Other North Vietnamese units which had not been involved in the battle remained poised in remote mountain retreats or just across the border.

Late in August the 324B Division of the North Vietnamese Army returned to Quang Tri Province, positioning itself deep in the jungles of the western mountains. The Marines countered with Operation PRAIRIE, an extensive project designed to check the threat of another Communist move into the populated eastern region.

By October the marines had been forced to shift more of their forces north to the demilitarized area. Third Marine Division Headquarters was moved from Da Nang to Phu Bai near Hue with a forward commmand post at Dong Ha while the First Marine Division was stretched to cover all of I Corps south of Thua Thien.

HEADQUARTERS, TASK FORCE OREGON, AT CHU LAI

At this point the first U.S. Army combat units were introduced into the northern I Corps Tactical Zone. They consisted of several batteries with 175-mm. guns and 105-mm. self-propelled howitzers. These were employed to provide long-range fire support, bombardment into and across the demilitarized zone, or, in the case of the howitzers, direct support for ground troops. More substantial reinforcements would be needed if the northern provinces were to be held. The enemy had increased his forces in I Corps from 23 main force battalions in the summer of 1966 to 52 by the end of the year. General Walt, with his forces stretched to the limit and short of helicopter and logistical assets, was unable to do more than hold his own.

Planning for Reinforcements

During February and March of 1967 the level of combat rose sharply in the demilitarized zone area as the marines attempted to keep the enemy off balance. On 25 February General Westmoreland granted permission for the artillery of the III Marine Amphibious Force to fire against purely military targets in, and north of, the demilitarized zone. The enemy responded with a heavy artillery barrage of his own against allied fire bases at Gio Linh, Con Thien, and Camp Carroll.

At this point, with intelligence sources indicating another major enemy offensive along the demilitarized zone, General Westmoreland instructed the staff of the Military Assistance Command, Vietnam, to prepare plans for a task force of four U.S. Army brigades, later reduced to three, with their appropriate supporting units, for deployment into I Corps.

When the enemy made several damaging attacks on Vietnamese Army units in the La Vang area in early April, General Westmoreland decided that the time for reinforcements had come. Major General William B. Rosson was assigned as commander of the new I Corps Task Force, designated Task Force OREGON.

Task Force Oregon

The organization and movement to the north of Task Force OREGON are worthy of some attention as the first deployment of large army units into I Corps. On 19 February General Rosson assembled a small group of officers and enlisted men to provide the nucleus of a planning staff for Task Force OREGON. This group immediately began operational and logistical planning in close co-ordination with III Marine Amphibious Force and U.S. Army, Vietnam. As the newly constituted staff began its work, General Westmoreland sent the major subordinate commands specific instructions outlining their roles in the plan.

While the task force planning staff proceeded with its work, the units that were earmarked to become a part of Task Force OREGON continued their normal operations. As the task force component elements were identified and mutual co-ordination and liaison established between units and planning staff, the units in no way disrupted their combat activities or altered operations underway. This formation of a provisional infantry division in a war zone while the component element of the new division continued to fight the war was in itself unique, and reflected a responsiveness, resourcefulness, and flexibility of Army leadership in meeting battlefield contingencies.

The brigades initially selected were the 1st Brigade, 101st Airborne Division, the 196th Light Infantry Brigade, and the 3d Brigade, 25th Infantry Division. The units had varying times of between 24 and 48 hours in which to assemble at different locations.

The provisional division was tailored to have basically the same capabilities as a standard infantry division. For simplicity in organization and ease in formation of the task force, the designated brigades with their organic battalions, separate companies, and detachments were adopted intact. Adjustments were made as necessary to insure that all capabilities of an infantry division were achieved. As an example, the 2d Squadron, 11th Armored Cavalry Regiment, was used as an infantry division cavalry squadron. Since the squadrons of the 11th Armored Cavalry did not have an organic air cavalry troop, Troop C of the 1st Squadron, 9th Cavalry, which was an air troop, was added to the troop list.

Similar steps to structure division support were taken by the planners in artillery and aviation. Engineer support requirements were met by combining the direct support engineer companies of each brigade with general engineer support increments from a combat engineer battalion. A provisional signal support battalion was also constructed by combining organic elements with attachments from the 1st Signal Brigade. The planning staff provision of military intelligence and military police support units followed the same pattern.

A unique method was used to establish combat service support for the provisional division. While an intact combat brigade could be taken out of an existing division, it was not feasible to lift a support command from a division, leaving the division without needed support. Fortunately the two independent brigades in the task force had their own organic division support, but there were no separate division size support commands available for inclusion in the new organization. As a result a tailored task force support command was created.

The units for the support command were drawn mainly from organizations, personnel, and equipment of the 1st Logistical Command. While these units were on duty with the task force, they lost their identity as 1st Logistical Command units and became Task Force OREGON troops. As such, they introduced several innovations, notably in the medical and aircraft maintenance areas, in providing logistical support for the task force.

The backup support to the task force, other than aircraft maintenance, was provided by the 1st Logistical Command through a general support group in the Chu Lai area. This group provided supply, maintenance, medical, and transportation support. When a brigade was to operate away from the Chu Lai base area, a forward support element was provided by the support group of the 1st Logistical Command. This command became the link with existing naval and Marine support elements in the area. Colonel Robert B. Pridgen, Commander of the Task Force Support Command, was responsible for providing backup support for the brigade and direct support to all the units comprising the task force base other than the brigades.

The area selected to receive the task force already had a well-developed support complex that was capable of supporting the 30,000 troops expected to be located in the Chu Lai area. The facilities included an airstrip able to handle jets; four ramps for landing ships, tank (LST's) ; three ramps for landing ships, utility (LSU's) ; a barge discharge pier; and a pipe line for off-shore discharge of petroleum, oils, and lubricants. The Duc Pho area to the south was less well equipped. This southern portion of the Task Force OREGON area of operation lacked an airfield to handle the C–130, adequate landlines of communications, and sufficient beach and pier facilities. Since these limiting factors were noted during initial planning, only smaller-sized forces were assigned to the Duc Pho area until the difficulties could be surmounted.

Deployment of the task force to I Corps began on 12 April. The predesignated units and individuals of the task force assembled at specified airfields and ports for final equipping and preparation for transportation north. The deployment was made by battalion combat team increments to the Chu Lai airfield. The heavier equipped units proceeded by sea to the Chu Lai port. The Air Force provided C–130 sorties and the Navy furnished LST's. Careful scheduling paid off in the orderly and systematic arrival of many different units and increments from multiple departure points in II and III Corps Tactical Zones.

The deployment of the Army's Task Force OREGON to the southern part of I Corps permitted the marines to concentrate their forces further north where the enemy build-up was becoming ominous. On 26 April, the Commanding General, 1st Marine Division, turned over responsibility for the defense of the Chu Lai Airbase and logistics complex with the surrounding tactical area of responsibility to General Rosson, the Commanding General of Task Force OREGON.

Continuing Activity Along The Demilitarized Zone

As Army reinforcements deployed into southern I Corps, more and more Marine units were shifted north. Bases and logistical facilities in the demilitarized zone region were rapidly developed and expanded. Dong Ha, the largest of these installations, served as the command and control center for operations along the demilitarized zone. Eight miles southwest of Dong Ha was Camp Carroll, a large artillery base. Another smaller artillery base was located at the Rock Pile, ten miles west of Camp Carroll. Both of

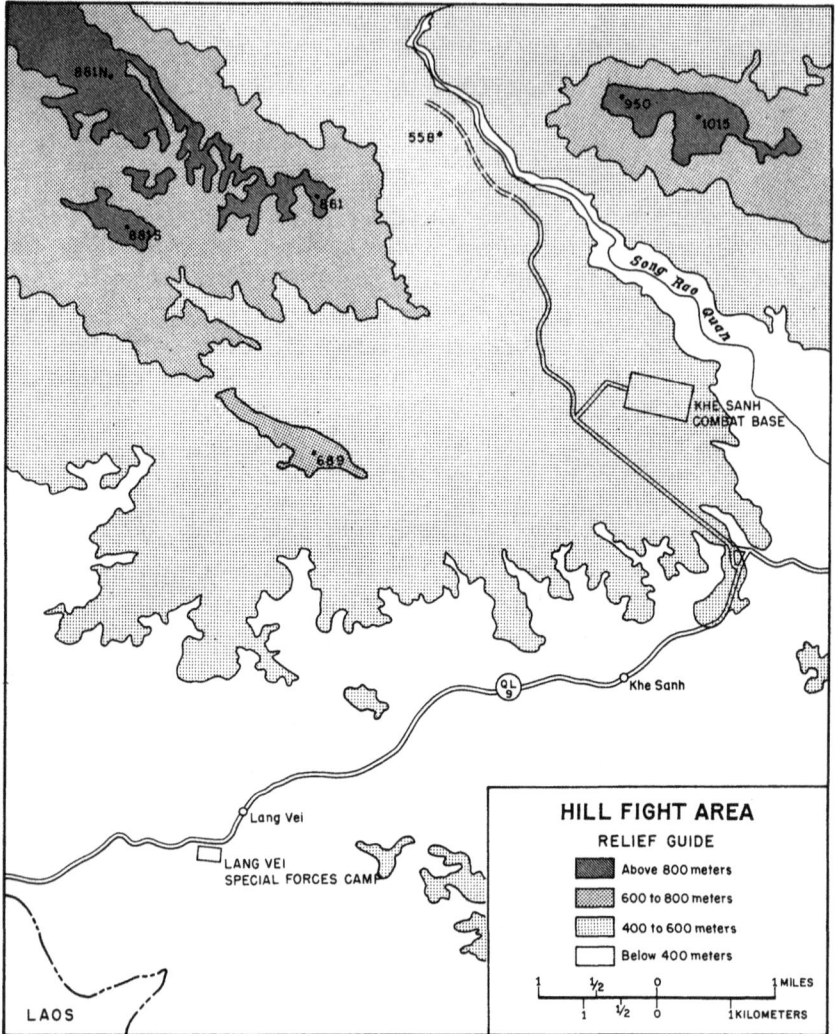

MAP 3

these bases supported batteries of U.S. Army 175-mm. guns. The western anchor of the defense line was the Khe Sanh Combat Base near Dong Tri Mountain in the formidable Annamite Mountains. The principal eastern bases were Gio Linh and Con Thien just south of the Ben Hai River.

Throughout the following year the enemy concentrated his efforts first on western Quang Tri, then on the east, and then again on the west. His initial efforts in Quang Tri province centered around the Khe Sanh plateau, ideal terrain for the North Vietnam-

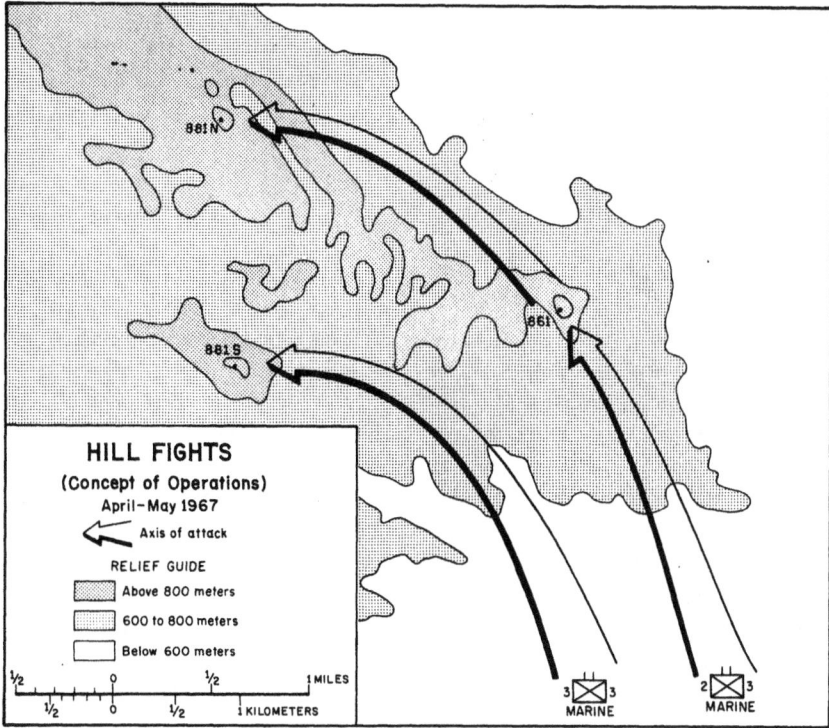

HILL FIGHTS
(Concept of Operations)
April–May 1967
Axis of attack
RELIEF GUIDE
Above 800 meters
600 to 800 meters
Below 600 meters
½   0   ½   1 MILES
½   0   ½   1 KILOMETERS

MAP 4

ese. The rugged mountainous countryside provided a natural infiltration route. Most of the mountain trails were hidden by three canopies of jungle up to 60 feet high, dense elephant grass, and bamboo thickets. Concealment from reconnaissance aircraft was good, and the heavy jungle undergrowth limited ground observation to five meters in most places. The most conspicious terrain feature is Dong Tri Mountain, at 1,015 meters the highest peak in the region. Four smaller hills—Hill 881 North, Hill 861, Hill 558, and Hill 881 South—dominated the main avenues of approach to the base. It was on and around these smaller hills that most of the significant battles were fought during the first phase of what was to become the long and stubborn struggle for Khe Sanh. (*Map 3*)

The battles began late in April when a Marine forward observer party became engaged with a large enemy force north of Hill 861. It is now believed that the marines prematurely triggered a major enemy attempt to overrun Khe Sanh. At least one regiment of the North Vietnamese 325C Division, it was soon discovered, was well dug-in in the vicinity of Hill 861 and was preparing to launch a ground attack against the combat base. In a series of hard-fought battles known as "The Hill Fights" the Marine units, supported by massive air strikes and artillery, pushed the North Vietnamese out of the hill complex. Losses on both sides were heavy. The 325C was badly hurt and for a time presented no further threat to the Khe Sanh area. (*Map 4*)

The Battle for Con Thien

The action now shifted close to the eastern area of the demilitarized zone near the town of Con Thien, located two miles south of the zone. Con Thien was a small defensive position situated atop Hill 558, ten miles northwest on Dong Ha. From this perch, the marines had a commanding view of any activity in the area. The position was never manned by more than a reinforced battalion but always had from one to three battalions near by which could be used to outflank any enemy attempts to storm the strong point.

Con Thien was to become the anchor for the western end of a barrier six hundred meters wide extending eastward some eight miles to Gio Linh. This strip was to be a part of the strong point obstacle system and was to be bulldozed flat to aid in visual observation. Obstacles were to be used to canalize the enemy and to provide protection for the various electronic sensor devices placed along the strip to indicate the presence of some type of activity. Strong points such as Con Thien were to serve as patrol bases, fire support bases, and stations for monitoring the sensors.

Beginning in May 1967 the enemy made repeated attempts to capture or destroy the Marine base at Con Thien. The marines countered with Operation HICKORY, a multibattalion sweep which soon developed into a number of fierce small unit engagements. The North Vietnamese opposing the marines were well-trained and well-equipped. Many were observed to be wearing flak jackets and steel helmets, and some employed flame throwers.

In July the enemy introduced a new weapon, the 152-mm. artillery piece. Fired from the demilitarized zone or from North Vietnam, it was the heaviest artillery weapon yet employed by the North Vietnamese. The marines countered with increased use of their own artillery, air strikes, and naval gunfire.

During September the enemy concentrated his attacks by fire against Con Thien itself. The shelling reached a peak during the week of 19–27 September when 3,077 mortar, artillery, and rocket rounds fell on the base. The Marine and Army artillery replied with well-executed counterbattery fire. This response, together with air strikes, appeared to give the enemy pause and his attacks slackened.

AERIAL VIEW OF KHE SANH IN QUANG TRI

Khe Sanh Again

While enemy activity abated in the east, it flared again in the western demilitarized area near Khe Sanh. During December, a surge of enemy activity in the area brought reports by Marine reconnaissance teams that large groups of North Vietnamese soldiers were moving into the area of the combat base. This time the enemy was not passing through but appeared to be moving in to stay. The number of clashes between Marine patrols and enemy units increased. The Marine companies that were dug-in on the outposts of Hill 881 S and Hill 861 reported receiving increased enemy fire, and Khe Sanh base itself was subjected to probes along the perimeter. (*Map 4*) Reconnaissance sweeps turned up evidence that the enemy was entrenching; many caches of enemy supplies were found and fresh foxholes located. Trails giving evidence of recent heavy use were discovered. The year closed on an ominous note, with more and heavier fighting in the offing.

CHAPTER II

Preparing For A Showdown

Before considering the climactic battles of 1968 it is well to consider several significant developments in the I Corps Tactical Zone: the project for an anti-infiltration system, the increasing use of other Free World Forces, the buildup of logistical facilities in the area north of the Hai Van Pass, and the upgrading of the Vietnamese Army in the northern provinces.

The Anti-Infiltration System

The anti-infiltration system, popularly known as the McNamara Line or Electric Fence, was envisioned as a 40-kilometer-long physical barrier supported by early warning devices and carefully selected fortified positions constructed on key terrain and manned as appropriate. It was intended to counter the massive infiltration of North Vietnamese troops and equipment across the demilitarized zone. The sensors, early warning devices, were designed to be used in a linear obstacle field. (*Diagram 1*) The balance pressure system would indicate any increase in weight, such as that produced by a person walking over it. The infrared intrusion detector operated in a manner similar to burglar detectors or an electric eye used to open the door of many business establishments. Unattended seismic detectors were used to note and report earth vibrations such as those caused by a group of men walking down a trail. Acoustic sensors transmitted the sound when men stepped on small explosive devices.

The majority of the firepower supporting the system came from artillery, tactical air fire, and naval gunfire. The system was designed to reduce the need for costly operations in an area constantly subjected to enemy-directed artillery and mortar fire from adjacent sanctuaries. The marines also hoped to use the anti-infiltration system to detect enemy incursions and movements at greater ranges. The system was an overall effort to counter both enemy infiltration and direct invasion by making enemy movement across the demilitarized zone simultaneously more expensive for the attacker and less expensive for the defender.

Work on the project began in April 1967. As the year pro-

DIAGRAM 1—LINEAR OBSTACLE

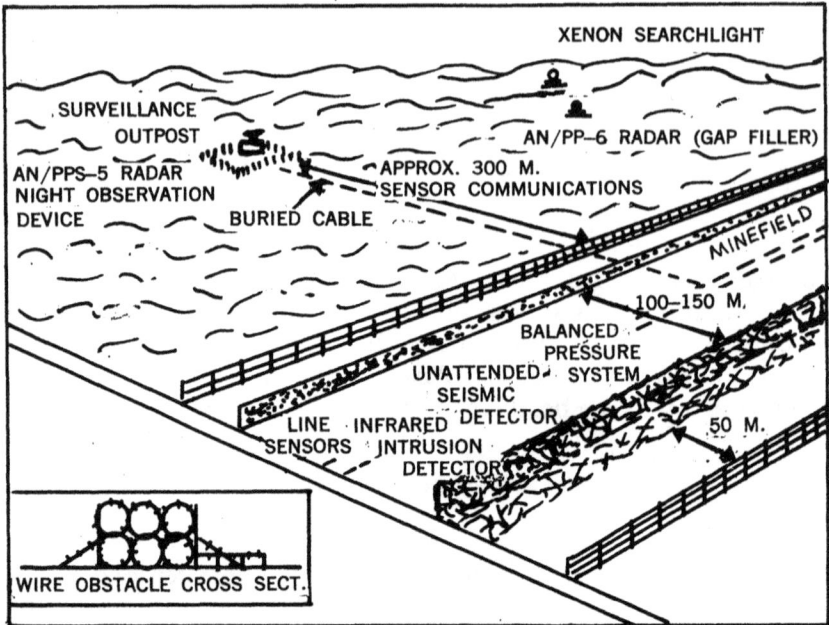

gressed, both the intensity of the enemy's mortar, artillery, and rocket fire and the changing military situation slowed down the development of the strong points and the construction of obstacles. The project was shelved when the buildup of U.S. forces in I Corps pre-empted the logistical support needed to supply the construction material.

Although the barrier was never completed, certain portions of it were sufficiently developed to permit their use. The defense positions along the line were turned over to the Vietnamese Army, thereby freeing the American troops for mobile operations. Some of the early warning devices later used during the siege of Khe Sanh were reported to be effective. The information derived from the sensors provided targeting data for bombing and artillery strikes. While alone no deterrent to enemy movement, they provided a portion of the information that enabled friendly forces to bring the enemy under fire. (*Diagram 2*) The monitoring devices could be dropped from planes and helicopters, hung in trees, placed along river banks, or buried underground.

In 1970 Congressional hearings were called to discuss the value of the instruments. They were credited with saving many lives by giving ground troops early warnings of attack. The sensors were credited further with increasing enemy personnel and equipment

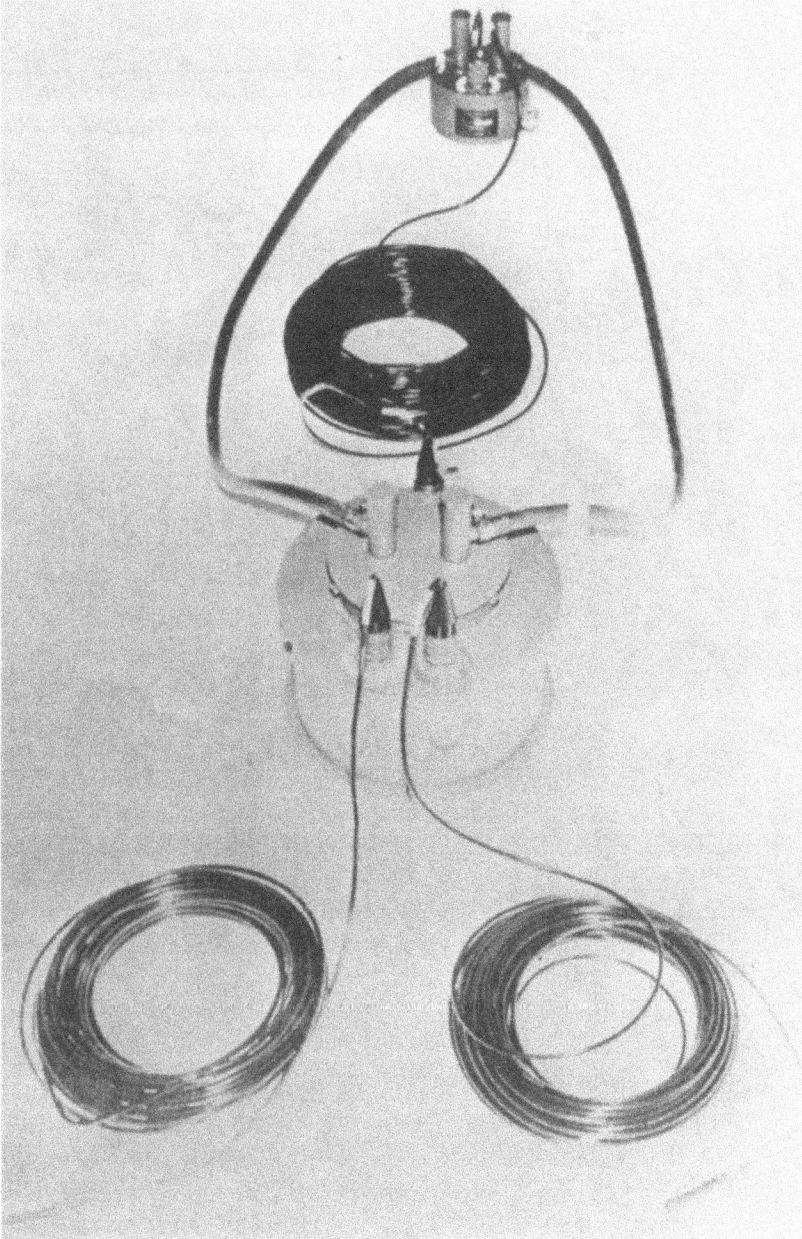

BALANCE PRESSURE SENSOR SYSTEM

losses as well as providing the Army with combat surveillance that worked by day or night. They were said to improve the effectiveness of air interdiction of enemy truckborne troops and supplies and to

DIAGRAM 2—SAMPLE TACTICAL APPLICATION

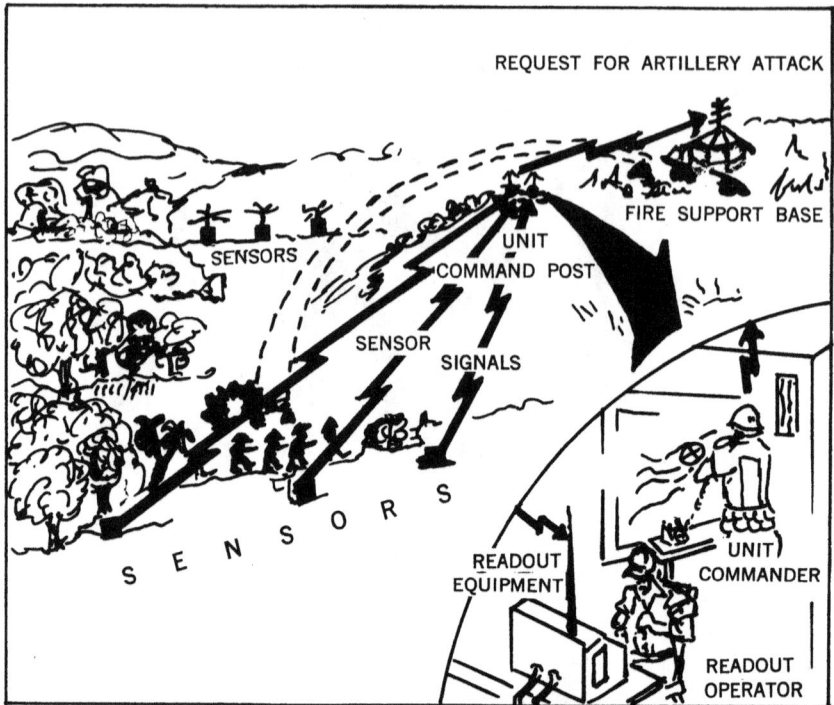

REQUEST FOR ARTILLERY ATTACK

FIRE SUPPORT BASE

SENSORS

UNIT
COMMAND POST

SENSOR
SIGNALS

S E N S O R S

READOUT
EQUIPMENT

UNIT
COMMANDER

READOUT
OPERATOR

conserve manpower. Some troop commanders stated that the use of the sensors permitted them to fight a major battle without the presence of their men. The sensors contributed to what was a difficult and, possibly the most important, task: finding the enemy and keeping track of his movements.

Free World Forces

Aside from the conventional U.S. Army organizations, other U.S. and Free World Military Assistance Forces contributed to the failure of the North Vietnamese to achieve significant success in I Corps. Among these were the U.S. Special Forces, the Vietnamese Civilian Irregular Defense Group, the Vietnamese Special Forces, the Republic of Korea Marines, and the Australian Advisors. (Chart 1)

The U.S. Special Forces in Vietnam were prominent in their advisory role in which they assisted the Vietnamese Special Forces in organizing, training and leading Civilian Irregular Defense Group companies on operational missions. These companies had

CHART 1—U.S. MARINE AND POPULAR FORCES COMBINED ACTION
PLATOON ORANIZATION

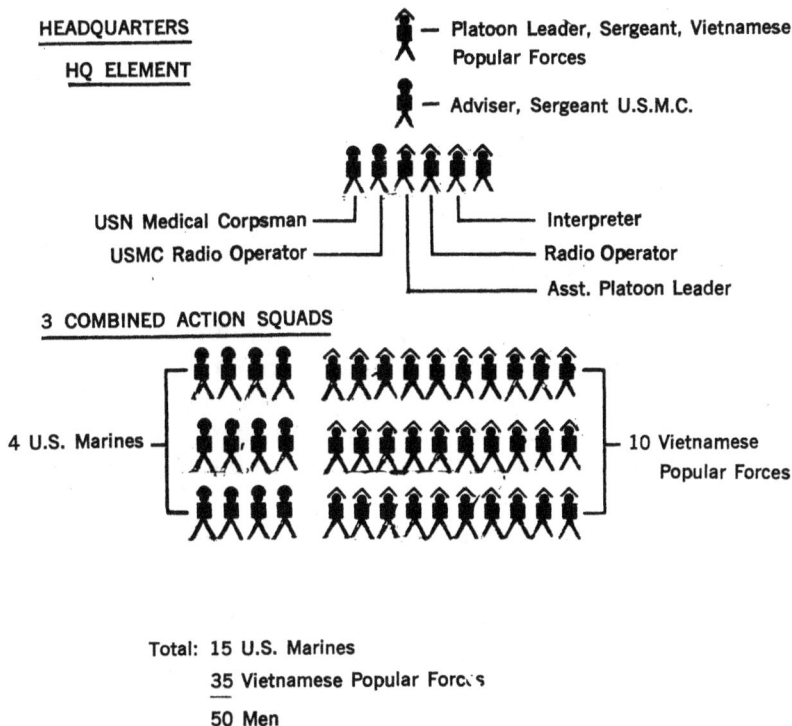

HEADQUARTERS

HQ ELEMENT

— Platoon Leader, Sergeant, Vietnamese
Popular Forces

— Adviser, Sergeant U.S.M.C.

USN Medical Corpsman ——| |—— Interpreter
USMC Radio Operator ——| |—— Radio Operator
                                                    |—— Asst. Platoon Leader

3 COMBINED ACTION SQUADS

4 U.S. Marines ——   —— 10 Vietnamese
                                                            Popular Forces

Total: 15 U.S. Marines
         35 Vietnamese Popular Forces
         50 Men

more than 3,000 men in I Corps and usually operated from isolated
Special Forces camps, like that at Lang Vei. The U.S. Special Forces
often provided the means of reporting enemy activities in sparsely
populated areas of the country. Not as well known were the U.S.
Special Forces' long-range patrol teams which roamed the areas
normally thought as being under enemy control. These teams provided much valuable information on enemy locations and activities.
On occasion they harassed the enemy by conducting ambushes or
raids in areas where the enemy felt himself secure.

After the United States, the nation which supplied the greatest
amount of assistance to the Republic of Vietnam was the Republic
of Korea. This aid was particularly significant in light of the poten-
tially explosive security situation that existed along the Republic's
borders with the Communist Regime of North Korea. It was also
indicative of the concern which the Republic of Korea manifested
for the freedom, progress, and liberty of its Asian contemporaries.

The Koreans entered I Corps Tactical Zone in August of 1966 when the Korean 2d Marine (Dragon) Brigade moved south of Chu Lai in northern Quang Ngai Province. Previously this unit had assumed the role of mobile trouble-shooter and had moved from its first location at Cam Ranh Bay to Tuy Hoa, then to the new zone south of Chu Lai. In 1966 and the following year, the brigade was in the vicinity of Hoi An, Quang Nam Province. Each time, the brigade's arrival in I Corps enabled the U.S. Marines to shift their forces further north where the continuing and increasing threat of invasion across the demilitarized zone existed.

The Koreans proved themselves adept in establishing rapport with the local population by stressing the kinship of aspirations and the "brotherhood" of the Asiatic peoples. Because many of the Korean troops had agricultural backgrounds, a natural kinship developed with the rural inhabitants of South Vietnam. Improvements in farming techniques and village accommodations resulted.

Korean forces conducted a number of the most imaginative and skillful operations of the war. They proved themselves to be masters in the patient collection of intelligence and in the effective use of it.

The Growth of Logistic Facilities

The development of logistic facilities had a great influence on the war in the northern provinces. The deployment of major Army units into I Corps in 1967 required the establishment of a support facility at Da Nang to furnish supplies peculiar to the Army. Eventually this organization assumed responsibility for Army support activities in Chu Lai and was required to establish a subordinate support command in the Phu Bai area with a forward support area at Dong Ha. In each of these areas, construction of troop billets, storage areas, roads, water supply systems, and various other facilities was required to provide adequate support for combat operations.

Before 1967, at General Westmoreland's direction, a campaign planning group had been established at United States Army, Vietnam, Headquarters. By mid-January 1967 this group had a contingency plan for troops, ports, roads, airfields, pipelines, combat support units, and service support units. The plan included requirements for a force about the size of the Free World Military Force that eventually deployed to I Corps. This foresight provided a detailed plan that was adaptable to the situation which developed in the northern provinces.

Logistic support in northern I Corps was dependent upon hazardous coastal shipping systems running north from the great

AERIAL VIEW OF HIGHWAY NORTH OF DA NANG

deep-water port of Da Nang to several shallower off-loading points in the vicinity of Hue and Dong Ha. The huge quantities of construction material required to build fortifications south of the demilitarized zone greatly taxed these already overloaded facilities and resources. To meet the existing requirements and plans for major operations in the A Shau Valley and other enemy base areas in the north during 1968, the number of landing craft sites north of the Hai Van Pass was increased to 18 and tonnage capacity was increased ten-fold from 540 tons per day to 5,550.

A most ambitious road project was the opening of coastal Route 1 along its entire length from the demilitarized zone to Saigon. This undertaking involved a series of military and engineering operations by many units stationed along the route, first to secure the road in the various tactical areas of operation, then to replace destroyed bridges and repair damaged sections of the route. Major sections of the road in the Da Nang area of Quang Nam Province of I Corps had been secured in the spring of 1965, when U.S. Marine units first moved into the area. In the spring of 1967, the 3d Marine Division secured the section north of the Hai Van Pass in Thua Thien and Quang Tri Provinces. Meanwhile, in the southern provinces of I Corps, Task Force OREGON cleared the section running from northern Quang Ngai through Quang Tin and into the southern part of Quang Nam Province.

Upgrading of the Vietnamese Army Forces

During 1967, the role of the 1st Vietnamese Army Division in I Corps expanded. In an effort to assist the division in adopting a larger role and to assume increased responsibility, planners took certain steps to increase its firepower. Starting in September 1967, the 1st Vietnamese Division's firepower was supplemented by the provision of such crew-served weapons as the 106-mm. recoilless rifle, 60-mm. mortars, and the modern M60 machine gun. Later in the year the division was further strengthened by the issue of the M16 rifle. There followed a noticeable increase in the morale of the division. With this greatly improved firepower, the division could be counted on for a larger part in the battles in the northern zone. A regiment of the Vietnamese 1st Division later relieved the marines occupying a sector of the defenses facing the demilitarized zone.

The Vietnamese 1st Division was given priority for this equipment in order to increase its firepower and to minimize the number of U.S. forces needed in northern I Corps, where the war continued to intensify. In the following year, the same process was repeated with the Vietnamese 2d Division in the southern portion of I Corps Tactical Zone. When their firepower was upgraded in similar fashion, they in turn assumed a larger combat role.

CHAPTER III

The Bleak Picture

Beginning in December 1967, reports were received of massive enemy troop movements throughout the country and along the surrounding infiltration routes. The enemy continued to move his main forces towards Saigon, Da Nang, Hue, Khe Sanh, the demilitarized zone, and a number of provincial and district capitals. The number of terrorist incidents rose sharply, as did the number of times Army units made contact with the enemy. By January of 1968, the enemy was well into his winter-spring campaign which he had begun in October of 1967. Numerous reports were received about a major offensive to be undertaken either before or after *Tet*.

Early in 1968 Khe Sanh again became the focal point of enemy activity in I Corps. All evidence pointed to a North Vietnamese offensive similar to the one in 1967, only on a much larger scale. Various intelligence sources indicated that North Vietnamese units, which usually came down and skirted the combat base outside of artillery range, were moving into the Khe Sanh area to stay. At first, the reports showed an influx of individual regiments, but then of a division. The establishment of a front headquarters indicated that at least two North Vietnamese divisions were in the vicinity.

This buildup around Khe Sanh drastically altered the security picture at the base. The road over which the base received its supplies had been cut since August 1967. Enemy activity intensified, and because of increased use of antiaircraft fire, it was no longer possible for U.S. forces to fly-in supplies with immunity. The bulk of the 135 tons of supplies required daily had to be parachuted to the Marine and South Vietnamese forces defending the base.

The main enemy forces in the area were identified as the 325C North Vietnamese Army Division, which had moved back into the region north of Hill 881 North, and a newcomer, the 304th North Vietnamese Division, which had crossed over from Laos and established positions southwest of the base. The 304th, an elite home-guard division from Hanoi, had been a participant at Dien Bien Phu. In addition, one regiment of the 324th North Vietnamese Division was located in the central demilitarized area some ten to fifteen miles from Khe Sanh, fulfilling a supply role. In the early stages of the siege of Khe Sanh, the presence of the 320th Division was confirmed north of the Rock Pile within easy reinforcing distance of the enemy Khe Sanh forces. The 304th and 325C Divisions were known to have armored units with them and were supported by the North Vietnamese 68th and 164th Artillery Regiments.

In other sections of I Corps Tactical Zone, intelligence indicated the presence of the 2d North Vietnamese Army Division in the vicinity of Da Nang, the 5th and 324B Division in the vicinity of Hue, and elements of the 308th and 341st Divisions in the northeastern regions of the corps area. For his planned attack on Hue, the enemy had an unhampered route and ready access to his logistical bases throughout the A Shau Valley. There were no Free World Forces outposts in the A Shau like that at Khe Sanh to the north in Quang Tri Province.

One of the many intelligence indicators of the vast increase in the movements of enemy troops was a U.S. Air Force report of truck sightings during the period. The reports showed that for the first nine months of 1967 there was a monthly average of 480 truck sightings; sightings surged to 1,116 in October; 3,823 in November; and 6,315 in December. This trend was in sharp contrast to the monthly average of 256 sightings during the final three months of 1966. The Air Force also stated that although enemy activity was on the rise throughout the southern infiltration corridors and tactical zone, the most serious threat appeared in the tactical area of responsibility of the III Marine Amphibious Force in northern I Corps.

During mid-January 1968, the undeniable threat in the Khe Sanh area prompted the greatest concern. Not only had the enemy positioned a large number of forces around Khe Sanh, but intelligence sources reported that Routes 92 and 9 in Laos showed signs of an increased logistical movement into that area, indicating the area had become a pivot point for operations leading towards Khe Sanh. While it was recognized that the disposition of enemy forces in the Khe Sanh area was a very real threat to the marines at Khe Sanh, it was also seen as an undeniable opportunity to direct concentrated air strikes against known enemy positions on a sustained basis.

Still another sign of reviving North Vietnamese interest in Khe Sanh appeared earlier on 2 January 1968 when a Marine listening post at the combat base reported sighting six unidentified persons nearby. A patrol dispatched to check out the unidentified men killed five when they failed to respond to a challenge. Later the five killed were identified as a North Vietnamese Army regimental commander, his operations officer, the signal officer, and two other officers. That these key men would undertake such a mission reflected high-level enemy interest in the base.

Operation Niagara

None of these developments went unnoticed in Saigon where General Westmoreland and Headquarters, Military Assistance Command, Vietnam, were monitoring closely all information as it became available. On 5 January 1968, General Westmoreland directed his principal operations and intelligence officers to plan for a massive aerial bombardment program to counter the rapidly increasing threat in the north. The following morning, Saturday, 6 January, General Westmoreland directed that the name NIAGARA be given to this fire support plan. The name was felt to be particularly appropriate because the support concept called for aerial bombs and artillery shells to fall in such volume as to suggest the falls from which the operation drew its name.

Two days later, General Westmoreland further amplified his instructions by directing that the operation be planned in two distinct phases. NIAGARA I was to entail a comprehensive intelligence effort to locate the enemy in the area of interest. NIAGARA II was to consist of co-ordinated heavy B–52 tactical air strikes on a round-the-clock basis against the located targets. General Westmoreland directed that the intelligence required to support this effort should encompass everything available from all sources. This support would include the resources of all United States Navy, United States Marine Corps, and United States Air Force strike, reconnaissance, and electronic warfare aircraft. In addition to normal ground intelligence-gathering activities, unattended electronic ground sensor devices were to be used extensively.

On 6 January 1968, while considering the plans for NIAGARA, General Westmoreland advised the Commanding General of III Marine Amphibious Force:

The anticipated build-up of enemy forces in the western DMZ area provides an opportunity to plan a comprehensive intelligence collection effort and to make preparation for coordination of B–52 and tactical airstrikes. We should be prepared to surprise and disrupt enemy plans for an offensive against Khe Sanh with heavy bombing attacks on a sustained basis.

Concerned as General Westmoreland was about that portion of I Corps immediately south of the western end of the demilitarized zone, he was all too aware that this was only one area where enemy activity was intensifying. Information becoming available at an enlarged rate indicated that a major enemy offensive within the next few weeks was a certainty.

In January 1968 the forces defending the Khe Sanh area included three battalions of the 26th Marine Regiment under the command of Colonel David E. Lownds. In addition to the maneuver

units in the Khe Sanh Combat Base, an impressive array of artillery
and armor was present. Direct support was provided by 4.2-in.
mortars, 105-mm. howitzers, 155-mm. howitzers, and 175-mm. guns.
These sixteen 175-mm. guns provided support by the U.S. Marine
positions at Camp Carroll and the Rock Pile. Five tanks having 90-
mm. guns for their main armament had been present since before
Route 9 was closed. Two Ontos platoons were also at the base. The
Ontos is a lightly armored track vehicle armed with six 106-mm.
recoilless rifles. These highly mobile vehicles could be rapidly
mustered at any threatened point. Originally designed as a tank
killer, the Ontos was primarily used in Vietnam by the marines to
support the infantry. These allied forces faced an estimated 15,000
to 20,000 enemy soldiers assigned to two North Vietnamese Army
divisions in the immediate area, a third division within striking
distance in the demilitarized zone, and a fourth one nearby in Laos.

Outside of the combat base itself, there were several areas of
tactical importance. The most critical points were the hill outposts.
Both Major General Rathvon M. Tompkins, Commanding General,
3d Marine Division, and Colonel Lownds, Commanding Officer of
the Khe Sanh Combat Base, were well aware of what had happened
at Dien Bien Phu when the Viet Minh owned the mountains and
the French owned the valley. They therefore considered it essential
that the hills around Khe Sanh remain in the hands of the marines.
Hill 881 S, Hill 861, and Hill 950 had been occupied by the marines
at the beginning of the year. This arrangement still left access for
the North Vietnamese to the Roa Quan Valley which ran between
Hill 861 and Hill 950. The regimental commander countered this
opening with the newly arrived 2d Marine Battalion. Hill 558 was a
small knob centered in the northwest approach. The regimental
commander placed one company on this hill to control that approach. Even with this unit in position, a flaw remained in the
northern screen. A portion of Hill 861 projected up to block line of
sight between Hill 558 and Hill 861. This stretch of high ground
prevented the two units from supporting each other by fire, thus
leaving a corridor through which the North Vietnamese could move
to outflank either marine outpost. This shortcoming was identified
and within a week a company was put on this ridgeline at a point
approximately 400 to 500 meters northeast of Hill 861. Thus, the
valley floor was under surveillance by marines from all the key hills.

The Battle of Khe Sanh—Opening Round

The Battle of Khe Sanh began at 0530, 21 January 1968, just
eight days before the enemy launched his *Tet* offensive. The North

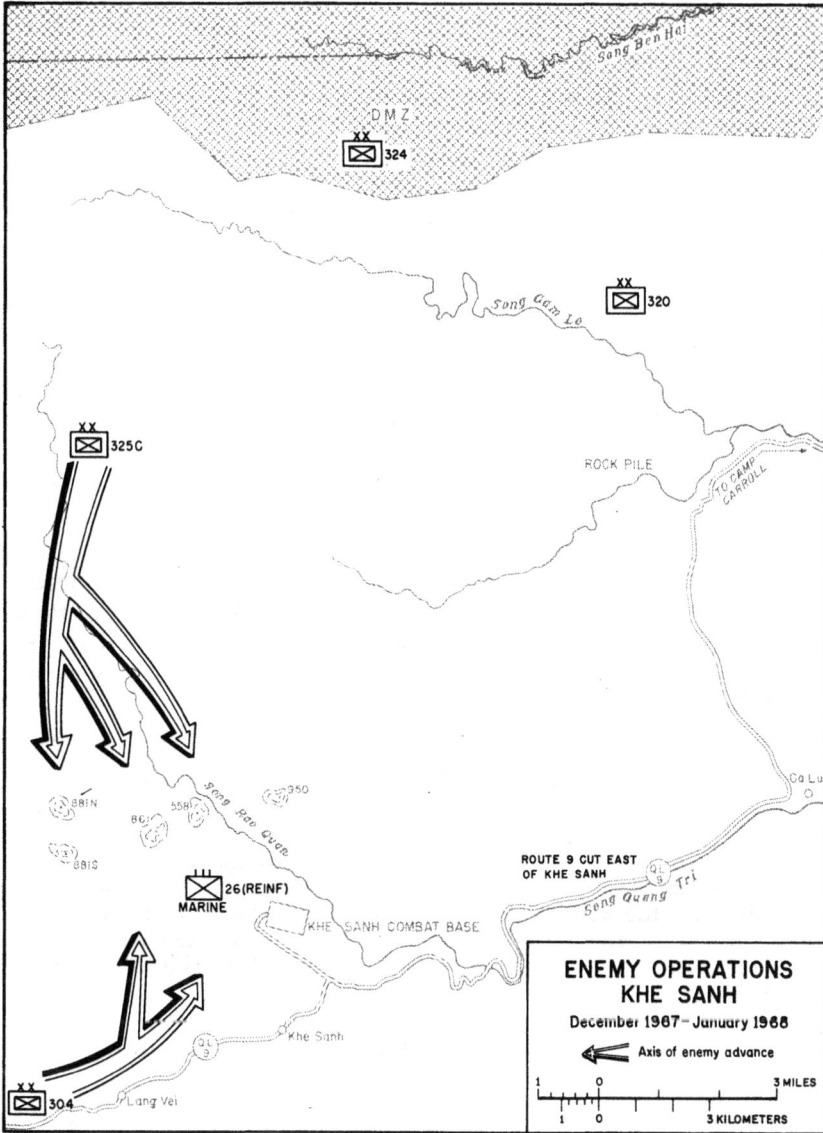

DMZ

XX
324

XX
320

Song Ben Hai

Song Cam Lo

XX
325C

ROCK PILE

TO CAMP
CARROLL

Song Rao Quan

Co Lu

950

881N

861   558

88IS

III
26 (REINF)
MARINE

ROUTE 9 CUT EAST
OF KHE SANH

Song Quang   Tri

KHE SANH COMBAT BASE

**ENEMY OPERATIONS
KHE SANH**

December 1987– January 1968

◄━━━ Axis of enemy advance

Khe Sanh

1   0   3 MILES

XX
304   Lang Vei

1   0   3 KILOMETERS

MAP 5

Vietnamese Army forces hammered the Khe Sanh Combat Base
with rocket, mortar, artillery, small arms, and automatic weapons
fire. (*Map 5*) Hundreds of 82-mm. mortar rounds and 122-mm.
rockets slammed into the combat base. Virtually all of the base's
ammunition stock and a substantial portion of the fuel supplies were
destroyed. The actions around Khe Sanh Combat Base, when

flashed to the world, touched off a political and public uproar as to whether or not the position should be held.

In South Vietnam where the decisions were made, General Westmoreland and Lieutenant General Robert E. Cushman, Jr., Commander of III Marine Amphibious Force, "after discussing all aspects of the situation, were in complete agreement from the start." The base, with its outpost, blocked the main avenue of approach into eastern Quang Tri province. The desired solution to the problem, using airmobile assaults in strength, was not possible owing to lack of both personnel and aircraft. Had they been available, the weather would have complicated such an operation before March or April. Not to be overlooked was the possibility of drawing a major enemy force into a position where it could be decisively destroyed. Another consideration in the decision was that the defense of Khe Sanh could be envisioned as a classic example of economy of force. It seemed certain that two crack North Vietnamese Army divisions which might have been used elsewhere in the province could be contained by one reinforced Marine regiment with a major assist from air and artillery strikes. In addition to these two divisions, two other enemy divisions, held in reserve by the enemy, were never committed because the situation failed to develop in the enemy's favor.

General Westmoreland had but two choices, to stay and reinforce or get out. He chose to stay. In his *Report on the War in Vietnam*, General Westmoreland told why:

The question was whether we could afford the troops to reinforce, keep them supplied by air, and defeat an enemy far superior in numbers as we waited for the weather to clear, built forward bases, and made other preparations for an overland relief expedition. I believed we could do all these things. With the concurrence of the III Marine Amphibious Commander, LTG Robert E. Cushman, Jr., I made the decision to reinforce and hold the area while destroying the enemy with our massive firepower and to prepare for offensive operations when the weather became favorable.

Meanwhile, at Khe Sanh, the battle was progressing. On 22 January, enemy mortar fire was placed on Khe Sanh and Hill 881. The enemy firing positions were in turn taken under fire by tactical air and ground artillery. Two resupply helicopters and an Air Force fighter-bomber were lost to enemy ground fire. To the west, across the Laotian border, an enemy force of three battalions assaulted and overran a friendly Laotian unit positioned astride Route 9.

The enemy attack against the Laotian position had been supported by seven armored vehicles which had approached along the road. Such a target would normally have received priority effort for destruction by air, but the weather would not permit it. A flareship, a forward air controller, and two B–57s circled the position attempting to get a clear enough view of the action on the ground to hit the attackers. The forward air controller described the weather: "The scene was low overcast, probably up to around 2,000 to 3,000 feet solid, with high overcast based at about 12,000 feet or so. We were unable to work visually in the area at all . . . ."

The Laotian troops, their families, and other local inhabitants evacuated the overrun position and withdrew to the east. They eventually reached the Special Forces camp at Lang Vei where the soldiers were added to the defensive effort. Although the commander of the Laotians had been a reliable source of information for some time prior to the attack, his report that tanks were a part of the attacking force was not accepted. Tracks of some type of vehicles could be observed from the air, but the weather prevented confirmation of the presence of tanks.

Also on 22 January, the 1st Battalion, 9th Marines, was moved into the Khe Sanh area and instructed to establish positions 1500 meters southwest of the landing strip at a rock quarry. Five days later, the final battalion allotted to Khe Sanh reported for duty. This unit, the 37th Vietnamese Army Ranger Battalion, was positioned along the eastern portion of the perimeter. At this point enemy activity subsided and remained fairly quiet for some days. The U.S. and Vietnamese forces, however, remained quite active, particularly in the air.

On 21 January 1968, the day the enemy attack began, General Westmoreland decided that the time had come to shift from the planning phase, NIAGARA I, to the strike phase, NIAGARA II and, accordingly, executed it. At 0930 the following day, the 7th Air Force reported the operation had commenced. Aerial bombardment and resupply became the heart of the defensive plan for Khe Sanh.

At the same time General Westmoreland ordered the initiation of NIAGARA II, the other actions were being taken to strengthen the Free World Force's position in northern I Corps. The 1st Cavalry Division (Airmobile) moved a forward command post to the vicinity of Phu Bai, ten kilometers south of Hue, on Route 1. The same day that the 7th Air Force announced the start of NIAGARA, the 1st Cavalry Division (Airmobile) Headquarters arrived at Phu Bai and opened for business under the operational control of the III Marine Amphibious Force. This timely reinforcement provided the commander of the III Marine Amphibious Forces with the necessary forces to subsequently thwart the enemy's major objective of capturing the cities of Hue and Quang Tri.

CHART 2—KHE SANH TASK FORCE
JANUARY—MARCH 1966

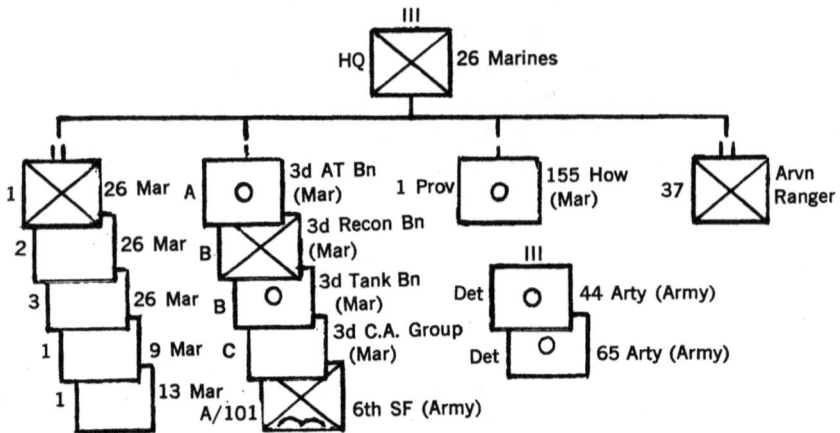

HQ | III | 26 Marines

1 | 26 Mar
2 | 26 Mar
3 | 26 Mar
1 | 9 Mar
1 | 13 Mar

A | 3d AT Bn (Mar)
B | 3d Recon Bn (Mar)
B | 3d Tank Bn (Mar)
C | 3d C.A. Group (Mar)
A/101 | 6th SF (Army)

1 Prov

155 How (Mar)

Det | 44 Arty (Army)
Det | 65 Arty (Army)

37 | Arvn Ranger

MAJOR COMBAT ELEMENTS AT KHE SANH COMBAT BASE

In further reaction to the enemy buildup in northern I Corps, on 25 January General Westmoreland directed the establishment of a Military Assistance Command Vietnam Forward Command Post in the I Corps area as soon as possible (The role this headquarters played in subsequent events is described in Chapter IV.)

As January drew to a close, the Free World Forces at Khe Sanh took stock. (*Chart 2*) All three battalions of the 26th Marine Regiment were present. The 1st Battalion, 9th Marines, 1st Battalion, 13th Marines, and the 37th Vietnamese Army Ranger Battalion were also present. A Civilian Irregular Defense Group company with its U.S. Army Special Forces advisers and the supporting aircraft control radar detachment representing the U.S. Air Force rounded out the 6,000 or so men in and around the base.

While the marines waited, they filled sandbags, dug deeper trenches, reinforced bunkers, conducted local security patrols, and in general established a pattern that would remain unbroken for the next two months. While the enemy did not launch a major attack against the Khe Sanh Combat Base at the same time as the *Tet* offensive, he continued to pour indirect fire into all of the U.S. and Vietnamese Army positions. Following *Tet*, during the first week in February, the North Vietnamese mounted three of its heaviest ground attacks. These fights on the hill outposts were extremely bitter. The North Vietnamese continued to prepare positions for their long-range artillery pieces as well as for countless smaller supporting weapons. They established numerous supply depots and began construction of their intricate siege works. This intensive buildup continued long after most of the fighting associated with the *Tet* offensive was over. During the entire time, the heavy enemy bombardment of the base and its outposts continued.

The Tet Offensive—First Phase

The most important of the Vietnamese holidays, *Tet,* began 29 January in 1968. The lunar new year season marks the beginning of spring and by the solar calendar usually falls toward the end of January or in early February. Work among the Vietnamese usually stops for the first three days of *Tet* and the festival begins with veneration of the family shrine and public worship. The entire population participate in celebrations, feasts, visits, and gay noisy public gatherings. *Tet* is traditionally a time of good feeling and family unity.

The Vietnamese in Hue and the surrounding areas planned the traditional celebration of *Tet* in late January 1968. A *Tet* cease-fire, traditional throughout the years of fighting in Vietnam, went into effect at 6 p.m. on 29 January. Many Army of Vietnam soldiers and most Republic of Vietnam government officials were on leave or off duty and enjoying the holiday season with their families.

After discussions between President of the Republic of Vietnam Nguyen Van Thieu and U.S. Ambassador Ellsworth Bunker, General Westmoreland took part in issuance of a joint declaration of a 36-hour cease-fire to be effective from the evening of 29 January through the morning of 31 January. Keenly aware of the ominous situation in the north, General Westmoreland made an exception in the case of I Corps where the increased enemy activity seriously imperiled the U.S. positions in the region. The Viet Cong, at the same time, announced a seven-day *Tet* truce to last from 27 January to the early morning of 3 February. Under the cover of this premeditated subterfuge, the enemy launched attacks of unprecedented scope.

On the night of 30 January, the North Vietnamese Army and Viet Cong forces violated the truce and struck many of the populated areas of South Vietnam. It was their largest attack so far—the infamous *Tet* offensive of 1968. The enemy attack was begun in I and II Corps twenty-four hours ahead of the attack in the remainder of the country. The enemy main attack kicked off late on the 30th and the early morning hours of 31 January, employing over 80,000 North Vietnamese and Viet Cong troops. Major assaults were made against Saigon, Quang Tri, Hue, Da Nang, Nha Trang, Qui Nhon, Kontum City, Ban Me Thuot, My Tho, Can Tho and Ben Tre. The

AERIAL VIEW OF SECTION OF CITADEL WALL IN HUE

enemy drive was successful in penetrating the cities in strength, but, in most cities, Regional and Popular Forces and the South Vietnam-

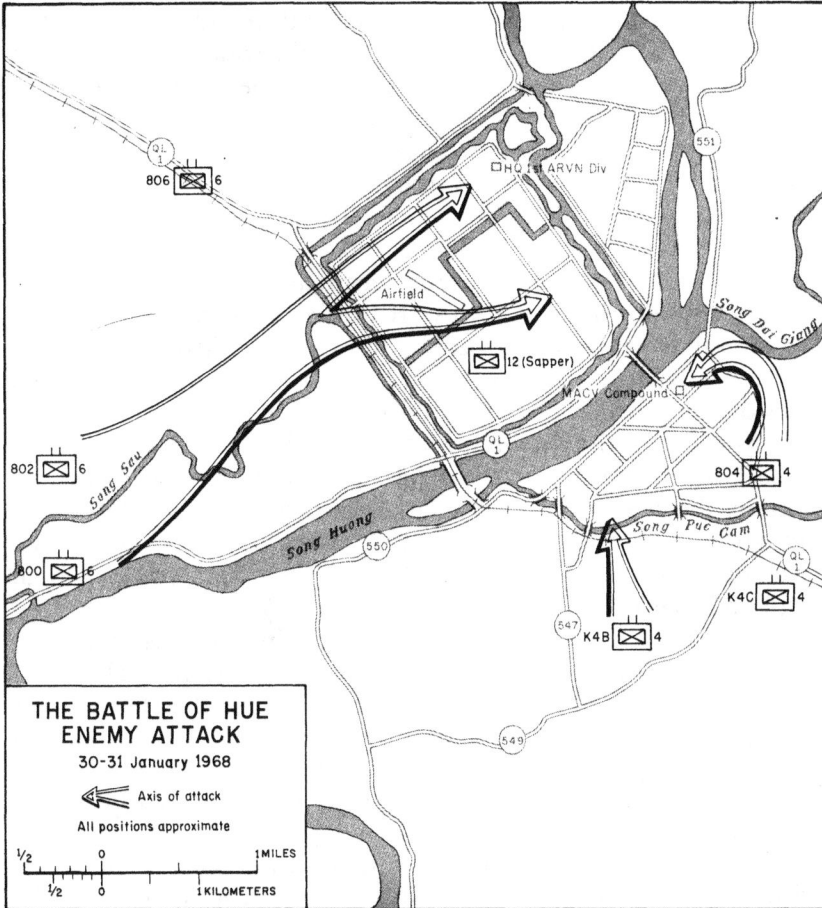

THE BATTLE OF HUE
ENEMY ATTACK
30-31 January 1968

Axis of attack

All positions approximate

MAP 6

ese Army threw back the enemy thrusts within two or three days. In some cases, however, heavy fighting continued for some time, especially in the cities of Ban Me Thuot, Ben Tre, Can Tho, Hue, Kontum City, and Saigon.

The Battle for Hue

Hue, with a population of more than 100,000, as stated earlier, is the third largest city in South Vietnam. It lies a hundred kilometers south of the demilitarized zone and ten kilometers west of the coast. The Huong or Perfume River, running from the southwest to the coast, divides the populated area. The Citadel, a walled city of about three square kilometers and comprising about two-thirds of the city, lies on the north bank, and the other third of the city lies on the south. A railroad bridge on the west and the Nguyen Hoang Bridge, over which Route 1 passes, connect the two sections. The Citadel is surrounded by rivers on all four sides. It is further protected by a moat which encircles perhaps 75 percent of the interior city. The moat is reinforced by two massive stone walls.

Because of the widespread truce violations by the enemy, the U.S. Military Assistance Command and the Joint General Staff of the Republic of Vietnam officially terminated the cease-fire on 30 January. In northern I Corps, Brigadier General Ngo Quang Troung, the commanding general of the 1st Vietnamese Army Infantry Division, improved security measures and instituted a series of alerts which placed his units in a state of increased readiness. As a result, the division headquarters in the northeast corner of the Hue Citadel was on alert on 30 January. At 0340 hours, 31 January, the enemy initiated a closely co-ordinated rocket, mortar, and ground assault against Hue. Attacking with seven to ten battalions, the enemy struck selected targets within the city, both north and south of the Huong River. (Map 6)

The enemy had carefully selected the time for his attack. In addition to the fact that most military units would normally be at reduced strength because of the holidays, the weather favored the attacker. The northeast monsoon produced foul weather which hampered resupply operations and grounded most of the air support which otherwise would have given the Free World Forces considerable help.

Under concealment of low fog, the enemy regular units, comprising both Viet Cong and North Vietnamese, were able to infiltrate the city of Hue with the help of accomplices inside. The troops quickly captured most of that portion of the city on the south bank of the Huong River and seized the greater part of the northern half including the Imperial Citadel. While the division staff of the 1st Vietnamese Army Division was on 100 percent alert at the division compound in the northeast corner of the Hue Citadel, only a skeleton staff of the U.S. Advisory Team of the Vietnamese Army 1st Division was on duty at 1st Division Headquarters in the Citadel. The remaining members were pinned down in the Military Assistance Command, Vietnam, compound in southern Hue by the initial enemy assaults. General Troung's action in northern Hue preserved the commands and staff structure of the division. Many of his officers who lived in southern Hue probably would not have been able to make their way to division headquarters once this battle started. Their presence provided a garrison sufficient when reinforced by the Hac Bao or Black Panther Company to prevent the headquarters from being overrun by the attacking enemy force. The Hoc Boa or Black Panther Company was an all-volunteer unit used as the division reaction force.

An enemy ground attack was launched against the Military Assistance Command, Vietnam, compound located south of the river in southern Hue by elements of the 4th North Vietnamese Army Regiment. Following the rocket and mortar attack, the 804th Battalion assaulted the northeast corner of the compound but was repelled by small arms and automatic weapons fire. A second attack made against the southeast corner approximately an hour later was also repulsed.

To the north of the Huong River, the 800th and 802d Battalions of the 6th North Vietnamese Army Regiment assaulted the Citadel. These two battalions drove from the southwest towards the 1st Vietnamese Army Division Headquarters. At four o'clock in the morning, the 800th Battalion was blocked by the 1st Vietnamese Army Division Hac Bao or Black Panther company at the Hue city airfield. After a brief engagement with the Hac Bao, the 800th Battalion was diverted south. The 802d Battalion was more successful, having penetrated the 1st Vietnamese Army Division compound and occupied the medical company cantonment area. The Hac Bao Company was called to the compound and together with the 200-man division staff drove the enemy out of the compound. By daylight, the two battalions of the 6th North Vietnamese Regiment, reinforced by the 12th Sapper Battalion, had occupied the Citadel except for the 1st Vietnamese Army Division Headquarters.

As daylight broke over the embattled city, the enemy had control of all but the northern corner of Hue. That is to say, the 6th Regiment controlled the population. The enemy had not attained his two objectives—the 1st Vietnamese Army Division Headquarters in the Citadel or the Military Assistance Command, Vietnam, compound. But in these two friendly pockets of resistance the picture was dark. The red and blue banner with the gold star of the Viet Cong could be seen flying in the Citadel flag tower.

Also among the holdouts were the scattered Regional Force and Popular Force units, though many were surrounded and cut off from friendly elements. Particularly important was the retention of the LCU (Landing Craft, Utility) ramp, and the 1st Signal Brigade's multichannel rapid relay complex. The former comprised the logistical key to the city of Hue; the latter, the communications gateway from Khe Sanh and Hue to the south. Outside the city, the North Vietnamese established blocking positions to stop any reinforcements by U.S. and Vietnamese Army forces to the embattled elements in Hue City. In southern Hue, the entire area

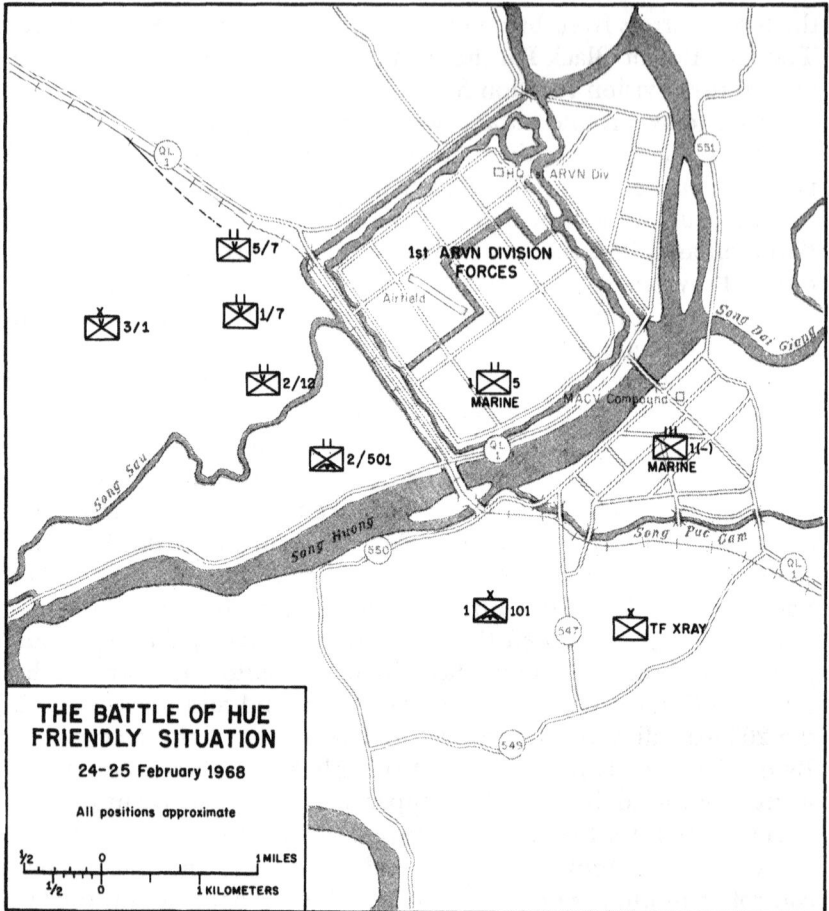

**THE BATTLE OF HUE
FRIENDLY SITUATION**

24-25 February 1968

All positions approximate

MAP 7

was seized and occupied, except for the Military Assistance Command, Vietnam, compound by elements of the 4th North Vietnamese Regiment.

Action was immediately taken to relieve the pressure on the two compounds. (*Map 7*) The 1st Marine Division committed units of the 1st Marine Regiment as a reaction force to aid the Free World Forces under attack in Hue. General Troung ordered his 3d Regiment, 1st Airborne Task Force, and the 3d Troop, 7th Cavalry, to move to the Citadel. Enroute these reaction forces encountered intense small arms and automatic weapons fire as they neared the city. The 806th North Vietnamese Army Battalion was occupying positions blocking Highway 1 northwest of Hue. The 804th Battalion with elements of the Co B, Sapper Battalion and the K4B

Battalion was in southern Hue. The 810th Battalion had established blocking positions astride Highway 1 leading southwest from Hue. The Free World Forces fought through these obstacles but again slowed as they encountered intense fire 700 meters south of the Military Assistance Command, Vietnam, compound. However, they continued on and reached the compound. Company A, 1st Battalion, 1st Marines, was the lead element enroute to Hue from Phu Bai along Route 1.

This company was followed by the Command Group of 1st Battalion, 1st Marines, which arrived at the compound at 1400. During the next three days, three more Marine companies, two Marine battalion command groups, and a Marine regimental command group arrived in the compound. A Marine tank platoon was also present. The marines made an attempt to cross the river on 31 January but were repulsed by the well dug-in enemy.

On 31 January, the mission of the marines was altered, giving the 1st Vietnamese Army Division, which was in an area on the north side of the river, responsibility for that area. While two battalions of the 3d Vietnamese Army Regiment moved east along the northern bank of the Huong River, two Vietnamese Army Airborne Battalions and the Cavalry Troop fought their way into the 1st Vietnamese Division Headquarters compound in the northeast corner of the Citadel.

On 1 February, the Vietnamese forces initiated offensive operations to clear the enemy from his entrenched positions inside the Citadel, and the marines opened operations to clear their area south of the river with particular attention to securing the landing craft ramp. The following day, the 3d Brigade, 1st Cavalry Division, moved into the operations area to seal off Hue City along the west and north.

During the early portion of the battle, the weather had been reasonably good. 2 February proved to be a turning point and conditions following that date became increasingly worse. The temperature fell into the 50's, which is quite cool for that part of the country. The prevalent misty drizzle occasionally turned into a cold drenching rain. As clouds closed in and heavy ground fog developed, it became difficult to use heavy fire support properly. Tactical air operations were severely limited and the majority of fire support missions fell on the howitzer batteries and supporting naval gunfire. Although less restricted by the poor visibility than aircraft, the artillery still had to be used with even greater precision. Even then the forward ground observers were occasionally required to radio corrections to firing batteries based on sound rather than sight.

During the period from 7 to 11 February the enemy units in and around the Citadel continued to offer stiff resistance. The 60 percent of the Citadel still in enemy hands included the west wall through which the North Vietnamese and Viet Cong were able to bring in reinforcements and additional supplies each night. The enemy was also using steel-bottomed boats to bring in supplies along the river.

The 3d Brigade of the 1st Cavalry Division arrived on 2 February and was assigned the mission of blocking the enemy approaches into the city from the north and west. The brigade had air assaulted into a landing zone about 10 kilometers northwest of Hue on Highway 1. They then worked their way south and east towards Hue. The men were tiring. As one trooper put it early in the battle, "We had gotten less than six hours sleep in the past 48 hours. We didn't have any water and the river water was too muddy to drink."

It was some time before the pressure was to let up on the men of the 2d Battalion, 12th Cavalry, of the 3d Brigade. On 4 February, the entire battalion conducted a daring night march through light mist and ankle-deep water towards high ground behind the enemy lines. At six the next morning, understandably exhausted, the battalion mounted their hill objective overlooking a valley still six kilometers west of Hue.

On 5 February, the 2d Battalion, 12th Cavalry, established positions on the high ground giving them excellent observation of the main enemy routes in and out of Hue. From that position, they were able to interdict all daylight movement of the enemy by calling artillery down on the plains below. The battalion remained in this location, restricting and disrupting enemy movement until 9 February. During the same period, the 5th Battalion, 7th Cavalry, was conducting search operations along enemy routes west of that area, then controlled by the 2d of the 12th Cavalry. On 7 February, the 5th Battalion made contact with the deeply entrenched enemy who had reoccupied the area from which the 2d Battalion, 12th Cavalry, had previously expelled them. Progress was halted by the stubborn resistance of the enemy at this point. The following day, the 5th Battalion, 7th Cavalry, tried again to breach the enemy's defense but was halted by heavy volumes of enemy automatic weapons and mortar fire. On 9 February, 5th Battalion remained in its position as a holding force to contain the enemy while the 2d Battalion, 12th Cavalry, left their location on the high ground and attacked northward toward their sister battalion. Enemy resistance stiffened as the battalion entered the village of Thong Bon Tri. Fighting continued throughout the day, and the infantry slowly moved northward.

As the fighting raged in the cities and towns and along the rice paddies and rivers in I Corps Tactical Zone, General Creighton W. Abrams, deputy commander of the Military Assistance Command, and General Cushman conferred on 8 February in preparation for a conference between General Westmoreland and General Cushman on 9 February. The result was the concurrent movement of the two battalions of the 101st Airborne Division into I Corps, one by air to Phu Bai to join the Marine Task Force X-Ray operating in the southern part of Thua Thien Province, the other by sea to Da Nang. The second battalion was tasked to secure the U.S. 35th Engineer Battalion as it moved north repairing Highway 1 from Da Nang to Phu Bai.

The South Vietnamese also increased their commitment to the recapture of Hue. Two battalions reinforced with the Vietnamese Army Cavalry Troop, 1st Division Reconnaissance Company, and the elite Black Panther Company succeeded in securing the airfield at Hue and then deployed south of the division headquarters in the Citadel. The following day, the remaining troops of the 4th Battalion and the 9th Airborne Battalion were airlifted into the city from Dong Ha and Quang Tri.

Meanwhile, the 1st Air Cavalry battalions remained in their positions through 11 and 12 February, blocking enemy routes and disrupting all visible movement by liberal use of artillery and airstrikes. On 12 February, the 5th Battalion again attacked the well-fortified enemy. By nightfall, there had been no substantial change in the opposing forces' positions. The cavalry battalions remained in their general locations until 19 February, conducting aggressive probes of the enemy positions and blocking the enemy's movement.

The 3d Brigade had been reinforced with the 2d Battalion, 501st Airborne, which began actively patrolling the vicinity on 19 February. Also on 19 February, the 1st Battalion, 7th Cavalry, was relieved from its base defense mission at Camp Evans and was deployed south to the area of operations on 20 February. The 3d Brigade, controlling four battalions by 20 February, continued to search north and south of the initial contact area and prepared to attack eastward towards Hue the next day. According to the brigade's plan, the two 7th Cavalry battalions were to push into the area of enemy resistance at Thon Que Chu, the 2d Battalion, 501st Airborne, would advance in the center while the 2d Battalion, 12th Cavalry, would advance northward with two companies held as brigade reserve.

During the night the four battalions moved into their attack positions and at the break of dawn on 21 February began their attack. The advance continued, with contact becoming increasingly heavy as the enemy contested every foot of ground. Air strikes, naval gunfire, artillery, and helicopter gunships helped over-whelm the stubborn enemy and permitted the advancing infantry to maintain steady momentum as they pushed the North Vietna-mese back. Before darkness, the battalions had all reached their objectives and were within five kilometers of Hue.

That night the battalions went into defensive perimeters, poised to continue the attack. On 22 February, the 1st Battalion, 7th Cavalry, remained in the battle area to search out by-passed pockets of enemy resistance while the other three battalions pushed their attack eastward to a point approximately two and a half ki-lometers from Hue. Heavy resistance was encountered in the after-noon but the battalions forced the stubbornly fighting North Vietnamese eastward as they continued their advance. Again on 23 February, the 3d Brigade pressed its attack and moved astride the enemy's avenues of escape from Hue. Throughout the day, enemy forces continued their stubborn resistance with mortars, rockets, and heavy automatic weapons fire. The attack was continued on 24 February against the desperate but weakening enemy forces.

The marines had been conducting clearing operations through-out southeast Hue. Marine elements, after securing the area around the Military Assistance Command, Vietnam, compound had fanned out east and west along the southern bank of the river. The 2d Battalion, 5th Marines, moved west then south, destroying bridges over the Phu Cam to prevent the enemy from using them as a means to enter the area. Although additional sweeps were con-ducted south of Hue, on 10 February, the area south of the river was declared secure. The marines then concentrated on the area north of the river.

On 12 February the marines displaced the 1st Battalion, 5th Marines, across the river by helicopters and LCU's. This battalion relieved the 1st Vietnamese Airborne Task Force in the south-eastern section of the Citadel. At the same time, two battalions of Vietnamese marines moved into the southwest corner of the Citadel with the mission to sweep east. The buildup of friendly forces in the walled city added pressure on the enemy, who in turn doubled his efforts to accomplish his own mission. From 13 to 22 February the battle swayed back and forth as the U.S. marines, Vietnamese marines, and Vietnamese Army 1st Division bore down on the North Vietnamese and Viet Cong within Hue. Ground artillery and U.S. naval gunfire were used in heavy measure to support the U.S. and Vietnamese combat force efforts to drive the enemy out of well-entrenched positions within the city.

During the period 17–22 February, additional pressure was brought to bear against the enemy. The 3d Brigade, 1st Cavalry, continued to press in from the west. On 19 February, the commanding general of the 1st Marine Division's Task Force X-Ray was given responsibility for co-ordination of all fire support in the city. Two days later, the 1st Cavalry Division's area of operation was extended south to the Huong River and east to the western wall of the Citadel. As the Cavalry moved to fill this area, they effectively cut off the remaining major enemy supply route and precipitated a rapid deterioration of the enemy's strength.

During the night of 23–24 February, the 2d Battalion, 3d Vietnamese Regiment, executed a surprise night attack westward along the wall in the southeastern section of the Citadel. The enemy was knocked off balance by the attack but once it began, he fought savagely. The South Vietnamese persisted and never lost the momentum their surprise action had given them. During the night they forced the North Vietnamese to pull back. Included in the ground regained that night was the plot upon which stood the Citadel flag pole. At 0500 on the 24th, the yellow and red flag of South Vietnam replaced the Viet Cong banner which had flown from the flag pole for twenty-five days.

At 0500 the next morning, following a thorough artillery preparation, the final enemy position was overrun. With the loss of this last toehold in the southwest corner of the Citadel, the remnants of the ten battalion enemy force that had attacked and seized the city either fled or became casualties. The Citadel was secure, and the battle of Hue was officially over.

During the relief of the siege of Hue, the forward headquarters of the Military Assistance Command, Vietnam, considered directing the commanding general of the 1st Air Cavalry Division to establish a forward command post in the city of Hue, co-located with the embattled headquarters of General Troung, commanding general of the 1st Vietnam Army Division. The objective was to establish within the city a major U.S. headquarters with sufficient command and control, air mobility, and artillery resources to co-ordinate and apply the forces necessary to break the siege. Brigadier General Oscar E. Davis, the assistant division commander of the 1st Cavalry Division, was designated as the Hue co-ordinator for the forward headquarters and co-located with General Troung. General Davis was to assess the situation and recommend directly to General Abrams resources needed to recapture the Citadel. General Davis's recommendations to divert certain troops to critical areas, to co-ordinate air and artillery support, and to accelerate supply procedures were decisive. Within 72 hours of his arrival at General Troung's headquarters, the siege of Hue was lifted.

The recapture of Hue had been a particularly bitter fight. The

AERIAL VIEW OF RUINS OF HUE

battle had formed with four U.S. Army battalions, three U.S. Marine Corps battalions, and eleven Vietnamese battalions on one side and ten North Vietnamese and Viet Cong battalions on the other. It involved house-to-house fighting similar to that in Europe a quarter of a century before. There was extensive damage to the city where some 116,000 civilians became homeless. It was an expensive battle in terms of human life. The enemy lost 5,000 soldiers within the city and an additional 3,000 in the surrounding clashes.

An extremely harsh price was the loss of life among the civilian population. This loss was the direct result of a systematic selection process followed by the Communists during the 26 days they occupied the city. In the wake of the offensive 5,800 civilians were dead or missing. More than 2,800 of these persons were found in single or mass graves during the months following the attack. Many of these victims were chosen because of their positions and loyalty to the Saigon government. As General Westmoreland pointed out, "This was a terrifying indication of what well might occur should the Communists succeed in gaining control of South Vietnam."

Intelligence

As the battle for Hue developed, it became rapidly apparent to commanders on the scene that the 3d Brigade of the 1st Cavalry

Division had taken on an unusually large enemy force north and
west of the city. Numerous documents captured during the action
indicated the presence of elements of three unexpected North Vietnamese Army regiments and several local units of regimental size.
The profusion of varying documents revealed that the enemy was
using this portion of Quang Tri Province as a staging area for
actions in Hue. In the last days of the battle, prisoners were captured representing the 6th North Vietnamese Army Regiment, the
24th Regiment of the 304th North Vietnamese Division, the 29th
Regiment of the 325C North Vietnamese Division, and the
99th Regiment of the 324B North Vietnamese Division. Interrogation disclosed that the latter three units had begun moving into the
area between 11 and 20 February to reinforce the weakening local
forces. What was surprising was that each of these regiments came
from one of the enemy divisions located around Khe Sanh or other
demilitarized zone areas. Their presence in the vicinity of Hue had
been previously unsuspected. The aggressive actions of the 3d Brigade of the 1st Cavalry Division had seriously disrupted the enemy
plans not only in Hue itself, but quite naturally in those other areas
which supplied reinforcing units.

Shortly after the opening of the enemy's *Tet* offensive, the U.S.
Army made an accelerated effort to obtain an indication of enemy
intentions through compilation of opinions of senior South Vietnamese officers. Possibly these officers would be more likely than
Americans to discern the thinking of their brothers to the north.
Named Operation LEAP FROG, the project produced information
acquired by a team of four U.S. officers who visited each division in
all four corps areas, except the 1st Vietnamese Army Division,
which was totally committed in Hue at the time.

Almost without exception the South Vietnamese Army officers
saw the attacks as politically rather than militarily motivated. Most
of the senior Vietnamese commanders felt the enemy was attempting to obtain a position of strength from which he could better
achieve his goals at any future peace talks. A smaller group of
officers saw the enemy objective as being the discrediting of the
South Vietnamese and U.S. military power to protect the population. With the exception of the divisions in III Corps, all commanders felt the offensive was an all-out effort using everything
available. Throughout the country, the enemy carried between
three and eight days of food, and many officers reasoned the enemy
intended to win within that time.

Another matter of inquiry was the degree of surprise gained by
the enemy in these assaults. Naturally, those installations not
attacked in the early morning hours of 30 January had the one-day

warning given by the first-day attacks. Many other Vietnamese
Army commanders had recovered enemy documents weeks, even
months before, that warned of attacks on cities in their area. There
were other general indicators of coming attacks during the *Tet*
period. Some units received agent, outpost, defector, or prisoner
reports in the hours immediately prior to the attack.

In some instances, although definite information was not available to accurately predict the time and place of enemy assaults,
prudent Vietnamese commanders had anticipated the likelihood of
such assaults and prepared accordingly. Already discussed was the
decision of the 1st Vietnamese Army Division Commander to keep
his division staff on alert in Hue—an action which contributed
significantly to the division's eventual success in repulsing the
enemy's savage attack. Another fortunate action was taken by the
Vietnamese 2d Division in Quang Ngai which called a practice
alert for the early morning hours of 31 January. Although apparently not called as a result of any warning, the alert had considerable effect in either delaying or disrupting attacks in their
area.

Further re-evaluation of the enemy situation led to the conclusion that the *Tet* actions were due a change in enemy objectives
resulting from the realization that time, once an ally, had begun to
work against the Communists. Intelligence analysts believed that
the enemy had developed two basic objectives as of February 1968.
Those goals were to win the war by a political and psychological
campaign and to gain and maintain control of the people. To accomplish these goals the intelligence people reasoned that the
enemy had set for himself three basic tasks. The first was to present
a constant threat in widely separated areas. The second was to
cause as many casualties as possible among U.S., Free World, and
Vietnamese forces. The final task was to gain military victories for
propaganda purposes.

To achieve these aims the enemy had placed the equivalent of
four divisions in the vicinity of the demilitarized zone. An additional overstrengthened division was located elsewhere in the northern two provinces. The actions at Quang Tri and Hue were
conducted by these troops in an attempt to regain control of the
population.

Battle for Quang Tri

While the struggle for Hue was the most spectacular battle of
the Tet period in northern I Corps, it was by no means the only
one. At Quang Tri City further north the enemy made a determined attempt to duplicate his initial success at Hue.

AERIAL VIEW OF QUANG TRI

Quang Tri City is the provincial capital for the northernmost province of South Vietnam. Like Hue, it is located on Route 1 about 10 kilometers inland from the Gulf of Tonkin. The city is positioned along the east bank of the Thach Han River some 25 kilometers south of the demilitarized zone.

On the evening of 30 January 1968, a platoon-size unit of the enemy 10th Sapper Battalion infiltrated the city. The unit's mission was to create confusion within the city by committing acts of destruction and sabotage while the main ground attack was being launched by the 812th North Vietnamese Regiment.

The enemy assault was to have started at 0200 on 31 January and accordingly the sappers went into action at that time. This of course revealed their presence and intentions. Fortunately, the ground attack by the 812th North Vietnamese Regiment was delayed because of difficulties imposed by the rain, swollen streams, and lack of familarity with the area. As a result, Regional and Popular Forces and elements of the 1st Vietnamese Army Regiment who composed the internal defense forces of the city were able to concentrate on the sappers before the main attack took place.

The 812th Regiment began its attack at 0420 on a multiple front. The K–4 Battalion attacked from the east, penetrating the city at several points. This battalion was to make the main assault and had the mission of securing the left gate of the Quang Tri Citadel wall and the province section headquarters. (*Map 8*) This

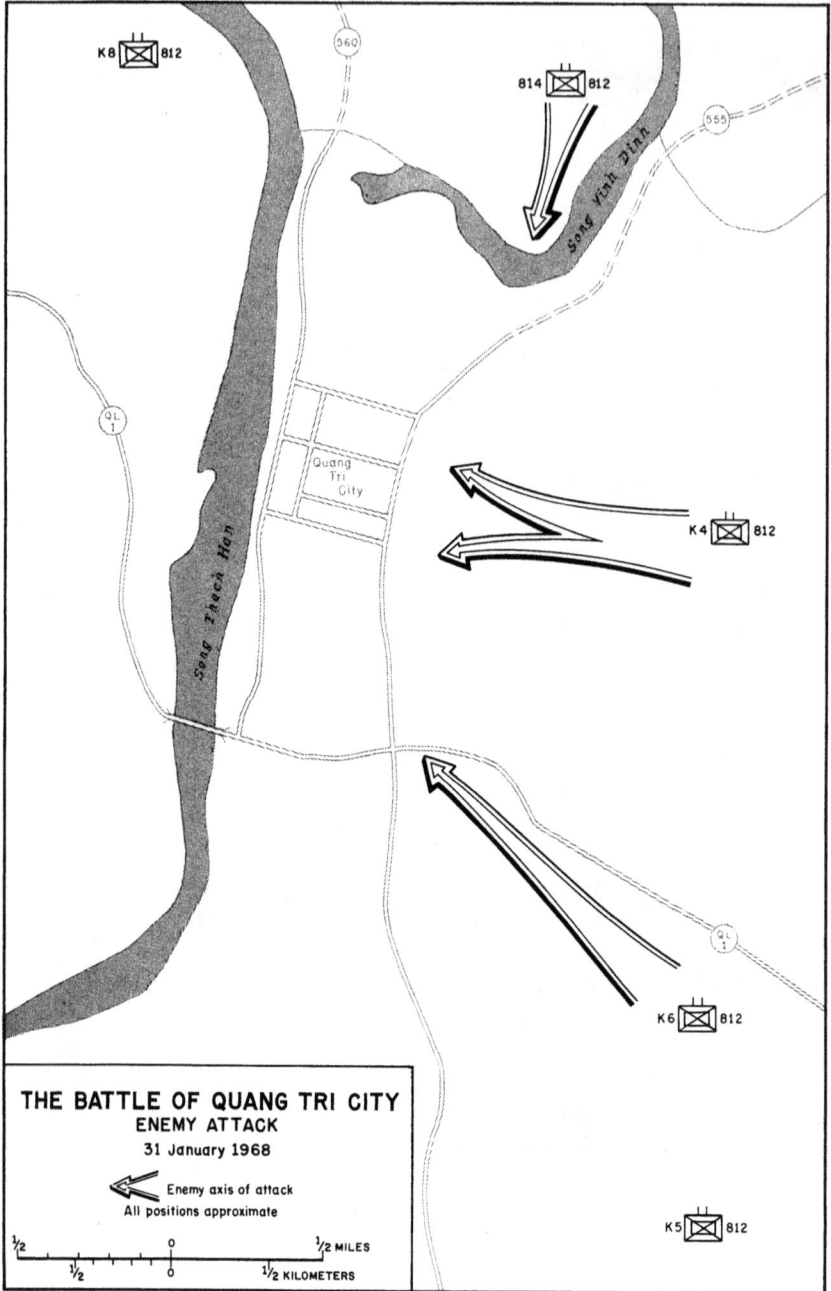

K8 ⊠ 812

560

814 ⊠ 812

555

Song Vĩnh Định

QL 1

Quang
Tri
City

K4 ⊠ 812

Song Thach Han

QL 1

K6 ⊠ 812

THE BATTLE OF QUANG TRI CITY
ENEMY ATTACK
31 January 1968

Enemy axis of attack
All positions approximate

½   0   ½ MILES
½   0   ½ KILOMETERS

K5 ⊠ 812

MAP 8

same battalion was expected to destroy the artillery unit within the compound and occupy the city prison.

The K–6 Battalion struck from the Southeast between Highway 1 and the railroad. The mission of this battalion was to attack the Vietnamese Army compound in the La Vang base area south of the city. The K–5 Battalion was the enemy's regimental reserve and was to occupy positions southeast of Quang Tri City.

The 814th Battalion, a Viet Cong unit assigned to the North Vietnamese Army, was to play a secondary role in the attack. Upon completion of the occupation of the city, it would occupy the whole city, allowing the remainder of the regiment to redeploy in a crescent formation on the southern side of Quang Tri to block Vietnamese Army and U.S. forces that were expected to come in as reinforcements from the vicinity of Hue. The fifth enemy battalion, K–8, also appears to have had a supporting role during the attack. Its mission was apparently to block Vietnamese units from reinforcing the city from the north and to reinforce the battalion committed in the northern portion of the city.

The brunt of the attack fell on the defending Vietnamese Army forces in and around the city. These forces were composed of the 1st Vietnamese Regiment, an attached Armored Personnel Carrier Troop, the 9th Army of Vietnam Airborne Battalion, and the police and Popular Force elements in the city. The 1st Regiment had two of its own battalions and the Airborne Battalion north and northwest of the city protecting revolutionary development areas. A third battalion of the regiment was located northeast of Quang Tri while a fourth battalion was in the city itself.

As the 814th Viet Cong Battalion attacked Quang Tri from the northeast, it was decisively engaged by the 9th Airborne Battalion and was unable to enter the city. However, the pressure on the defending Vietnamese Army forces remained heavy and, fighting for every foot of ground, they were forced to pull back into the city. Although the enemy had been unable to take over the city, they exerted great pressure on its defenders and at noon of the 31st the outcome of the battle remained uncertain.

The Vietnamese forces were not entirely on their own at Quang T i City. On 25 January the 1st Brigade of the 1st Cavalry Division, co nmanded by Colonel Donald V. Rattan, had been moved into th area from position near Hue and Phu Bai. Since 17 January, the brigade's mission had been to launch attacks into a known enemy base area located roughly 15 kilometers southwest of Quang Tri City. The brigade had an additional mission to block approaches into the city from the southwest but was primarily concerned with its offensive mission and accordingly had two fire bases,

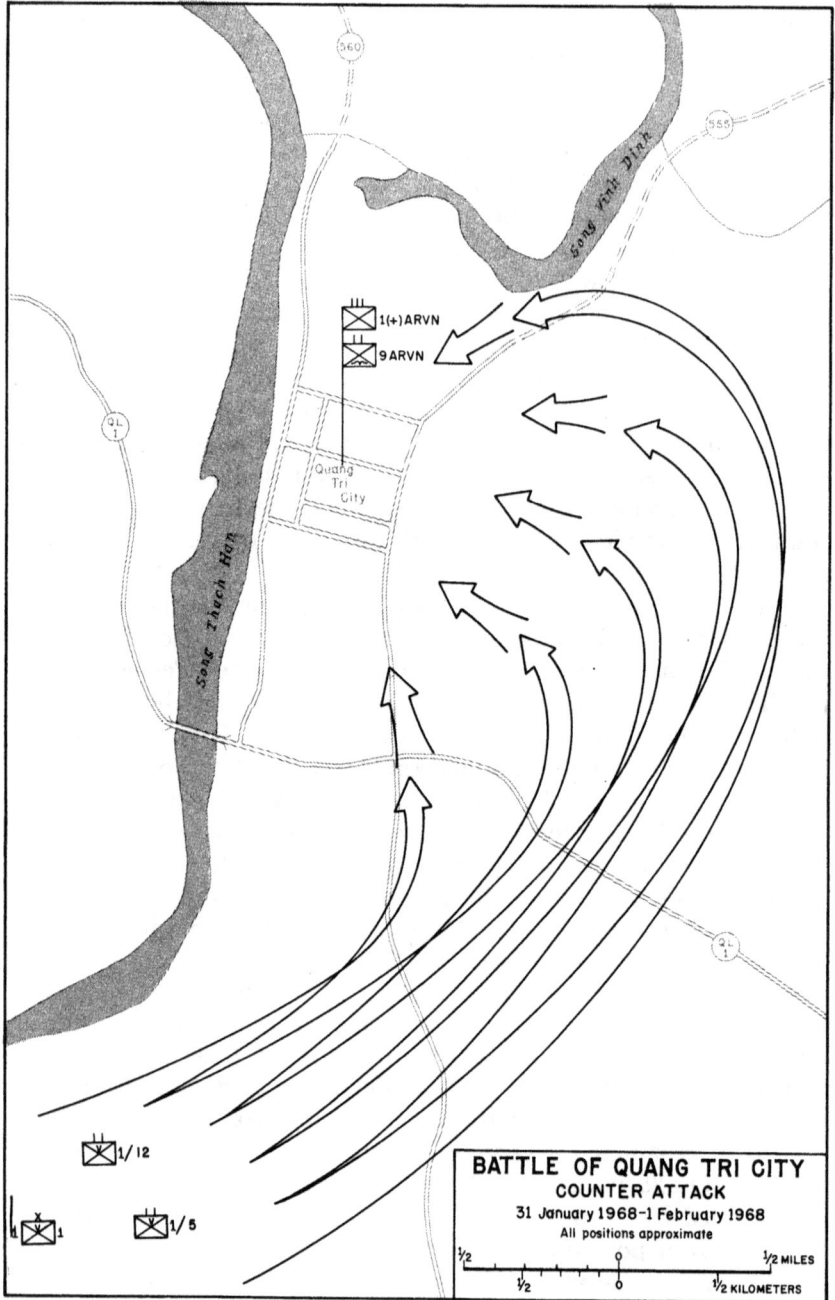

BATTLE OF QUANG TRI CITY
COUNTER ATTACK
31 January 1968–1 February 1968
All positions approximate

MAP 9

one 15 kilometers west of the city and one in the middle of the enemy base area. The action of the 814th Viet Cong Battalion redirected the attention of the cavalry troops.

Shortly after noon on 31 January, the senior adviser to the Province Chief, Mr. Robert Brewer, held a conference with the 1st Brigade, 1st Cavalry Division Commander, Colonel Rattan, and the senior U.S. adviser to the Vietnamese 1st Regiment. The situation in the city was still in doubt. The enemy had infiltrated at least a battalion into the city and its defending forces were in need of immediate assistance. At the time, it appeared that the enemy was reinforcing from the east and had established fire support positions on the eastern fringes of the city.

At the time of the assault, the brigade headquarters at Landing Zone BETTY and other landing zones in addition to the Vietnamese Army base camp at La Vang had come under sporadic rocket and mortar attacks. A dense fog blanketed the area. Despite these factors, the brigade was able to react quickly to the new situation. The 1st Battalion of the 8th Cavalry could not be moved from its mountain top position in the enemy base area because of the dense fog. Also, the 1st Battalion, 502d Airborne, of the 101st Airborne Division which was under operation control of the 1st Brigade, 1st Cavalry Division, continued its base defense mission and tactical operation just west of Quang Tri. (*Map 9*)

This development left only the 1st Battalion of the 12th Cavalry and the 1st Battalion of the 5th Cavalry for use against the attacking enemy. Each of these battalions had opened new fire bases to the west of the city, along the river valley leading to Khe Sanh, on 30 January. At approximately 1345 on 30 January, the battalions were directed to close out the new fire bases and launch their assaults as soon as possible to reduce the enemy's ability to bring additional forces into the city by blocking avenues of approach and eliminating enemy support. The two elements would also block or impede withdrawal of enemy forces already in the city. By 1555, the cavalry battalions had air assaulted into five locations northeast, east, and southeast of the city. Mr. Brewer's insistence that enemy troops were in these areas proved to be correct. The helicopters received intense enemy fire as they landed their troops east of the city. Contact continued until 1900 as the surprised and confused enemy fought with machine guns, mortars, and recoilless rifles. The cavalry air assaults had straddled the heavy weapons support of the K–4 Battalion, and the enemy battalion found itself heavily engaged on the eastern edge of Quang Tri by the Vietnamese Army and in its rear, among its support elements, by the cavalry. Caught between these forces, it was quickly rendered ineffective.

UH – 1B Gunship of 1st Cavalry Division

Shortly after the 12th Cavalry jumped, two companies of the 1st of the 5th Cavalry air-assaulted southeast of Quang Tri. They quickly became heavily engaged by the enemy. Another enemy battalion, the K–6, found itself wedged between the Vietnamese Army forces and the cavalrymen. The enemy sustained a terrific pounding from helicopter gunships and artillery as the 1st Brigade scout helicopters brought in aerial rocket artillery. As darkness fell, it became apparent that the shattered enemy had had enough. He attempted to break contact and withdraw. Because it was difficult to withdraw large units through the cavalry, enemy forces rapidly broke down into small groups, and some individuals attempted to get away among the crowds of fleeing refugees. Clashes continued throughout the night.

Through the 1st of February, the disorganized enemy units sought to avoid contact. They had suffered a terrible mauling from the Vietnamese Army defenders within Quang Tri and had been demoralized by the air-assaults, gunships, and ground attacks of the 1st Cavalry Division. Aerial rocket artillery and helicopter gunships experienced unusual success against the enemy troops.

By noon on 1 February, Quang Tri City had been cleared of the enemy and the 1st Brigade immediately initiated pursuit. Moving in ever increasing concentric circles centered on the city, 1st Brigade elements relentlessly harried the demoralized enemy. Numerous

U.S. ENGINEERS REPAIRING APPROACH TO BRIDGE

heavy contacts with large well-armed enemy forces south of Quang Tri were made. Other units of the 1st Brigade made smaller contacts. This pursuit continued throughout the first ten days of February.

The city of Quang Tri was without a doubt one of the major objectives of the *Tet* offensive. Three factors contributed to the U.S. and Vietnamese success: the tenacious defense within and around the city on the part of all of the Vietnamese forces; the timely and accurate tactical intelligence of the enemy locations provided to the 1st Brigade by the province senior adviser, Mr. Brewer; and the air mobile tactics of the 1st Cavalry Division. The enemy paid a high price for his failure. He lost more than 900 soldiers killed and almost 100 captured in addition to heavy losses in weapons, ammunition, and equipment.

Enemy Attacks on the Logistical System

Concurrently with assaults on Hue and Quang Tri City and his continued pressure on Khe Sanh, the enemy struck at the more vulnerable roads, bridges, and waterways used to supply the friendly positions in the I Corps Tactical Zone. While a reinforced regiment of U.S. Marines tied down three or four enemy divisions around Khe Sanh, two enemy divisions were in northeast Quang Tri Province and elements of three additional divisions were operating along the coastal plains from Quang Tri City south to the Hai Van Pass, stopping all traffic carrying supplies north on Highway 1. An 8-inch oil pipe line used to transport aviation fuel from Tan My to Hue was cut, and the 50,000-gallon capacity storage tanks at Tan My were destroyed.

The bulk of supplies shipped to Hue from Da Nang were moved by tank landing ships (LST's). These supplies were transported from the large LST's via the Huong River to Hue and via the Cua Viet River to Dong Ha by smaller utility landing craft (LCU). With the commencement of the *Tet* offensive, the enemy began a series of harassing attacks to disrupt the delivery of supplies over these inland waterways.

The only secure terminals for delivery of supplies were the airports at Quang Tri and Phu Bai. The full use of these facilities was prevented by poor weather. The U.S. forces were using 2,600 tons of supplies a day, excluding bulk petroleum items, and an additional 1,000 tons a day were required to reconstitute stocks needed for a counteroffensive to relieve Khe Sanh.

The logistic situation was critical. Military developments in northern South Vietnam required an influx of combat troops at a rate that, of necessity, exceeded the capability to create a supply base for their logistical support in an orderly and economical fashion. The fundamental approach to support in Vietnam was to have the Military Assistance Command, Vietnam, establish the basic policies for all services and to have each service implement the basic policy in accordance with the requirements for that particular service.

To economize as much as possible, planners also decided that support would be conducted on an area basis for all common supplies. In effect this meant that the Navy, which had responsibility for area supply in I Corps Tactical Zone, would provide common supply items such as food and gasoline. This basic decision remained unchanged although variation in troop densities among the regions caused occasional modification.

When the enemy opened his *Tet* offensive, he placed an additional burden on the U.S. supply system then extant in I Corps and already strained to the breaking point. Colonel Daniel F. Munster, a logistics officer for the Military Assistance Command, Vietnam, determined the amount of supplies his units consumed each day and realized he must have additional tonnage to reconstitute stocks and to build up for the counteroffensive to relieve Khe Sanh which was tentatively planned to begin 1 April 1968.

During January and February approximately 45,000 U.S. Army

troops had deployed into I Corps. Colonel Munster and his fellow planners had to provide 3,600 tons of supplies daily in an area where existing supply lines were just barely able to keep up with current requirements. Furthermore, this tonnage did not include bulk needs for petroleum, oils, and lubricants. Key decisions were made and implemented during a thirty-day period to stabilize the situation and prepare for the counteroffensive.

The first decision was that only essentials were to be brought in. As General Abrams observed, "Anyone who brings in non-essentials is interfering with the conduct of the war." This decision limited the use of the available means of transportation to moving only combat essential items into northern I Corps: only "beans, bullets and gasoline." P.X. items, beer, and furniture had to be deferred. Second, the important supply line closed by the enemy actions at the Hai Van Pass had to be reopened. This task was accomplished through simultaneous ground attacks from friendly bases along Highway 1 north and south of the blocked pass. The highway was then repaired and improved. A traffic management agency was established at Headquarters, III Marine Amphibious Force, in Da Nang to co-ordinate convoys moving north and south along this critical stretch of Highway 1. This activity was later moved to the forward headquarters of the Military Assistance Command, Vietnam, and renamed the Convoy Control Center. The first convoy to move north from Da Nang on the reopened road contained 155 vehicles and set out on 1 March 1968. The actual volume of supplies moved over Route 1 was less than satisfactory and the subject of concern to the headquarters of the Provincial Corps, Vietnam. The reopened road had a rated capacity of 250 tons a day, but engineering problems and shortage of cargo vehicles continued.

The next project of importance was the restoration of the fuel line from Tan My to Hue, and initiation of repairs on the 50,000-barrel storage facility at Tan My. Both of these requirements were accomplished, but most important of all was the establishment of a logistical over-the-shore or LOTS facility east of Quang Tri and construction of a two-lane road to connect the beach with Highway 1. The LOTS facility was a major accomplishment. Amphibious lighterage units, terminal service units, U.S. Army Transportation Corps companies, Navy Seabees, and a Marine Fuel detachment all worked together at top speed to produce what proved to be the key logistical facility in the area. A POL (petroleum, oils, and lubricants) line laid from the beach to Highway 1 and then north to Dong Ha became the principal supply line for the U.S. Army troops. Sea lines were laid to accept bulk POL; extensive ammuni-

A LARC – 5 COMES ASHORE

tion and fuel storage areas were developed; a helicopter refueling and lift-off point was constructed. Supplies of all types were brought ashore from deep draft ships by amphibious resupply cargo barges (BARC's) and amphibious resupply cargo lighters (LARC's). These large amphibious vehicles proved ideal for such work.

Tank landing ships (LST's) and other landing craft were discharged over a ponton causeway. Each day convoys of transportation truck units moved the cargo inland from the beach storage to the forward support bases of the combat divisions. Although originally some skeptical observers predicted that daily receipts would not exceed 350 short tons, the LOTS facility, later designated Utah Beach, often greatly exceeded this amount as shown below:

16 March	860	Short Tons
17 March	1252	Short Tons
18 March	363	Short Tons
19 March	1232	Short Tons
21 March	1862	Short Tons
22 March	816	Short Tons
24 March	1514	Short Tons
29 March	1000	Short Tons

The U.S. Army's 159th Transportation Battalion (Terminal),

LARC – 5 Operations Off Wunder Beach

commanded by Lieutenant Colonel Charles H. Sunder, was the
major unit on the beach. Because of the remarkable achievements
of the supply and transportation personnel of all the services on
the beach, the facility became known as Wunder Beach and the
men of the 159th Battalion as Sunder's Wonders.

An unusual occurrence connected with the establishment of

CARGO CRAFT AND PATROL BOAT

logistic facilities was the crossing of the North Vietnamese and U.S. main supply routes north of Hue in early 1968. The North Vietnamese main supply route originated north of the demilitarized zone and ran south along the coast to the vicinity of Hue. The establishment of a major U.S. supply point at Wunder Beach generated a supply route from the beach inland to the operating forces. Where these two main supply routes crossed, the U.S. efforts to keep the supplies moving interdicted the enemy supply route.

It was decided to improve the capability of the U.S. Air Force to handle larger numbers of troops and supplies at the Phu Bai airbase. The Air Force met this challenge by deploying longer-range navigational equipment and additional personnel. The marines also assisted by making emergency repairs to extend the runway, by increasing the number of parking ramps, and by improving administrative facilities. As the weather improved, air delivery of supplies increased. By mid-March supplies were being received in sufficient quantities to satisfy daily needs and build up stocks for the counteroffensive.

Task Force Clearwater

A vital part of the logistic effort in northern I Corps was the

RIVER PATROL BOAT

development of uninterrupted inland water lines of communication. The intense struggle for Hue underscored the importance of these supply lines. Logistic watercraft using the Huong River to deliver supplies to Hue were subjected to heavy punishment by rockets, automatic weapons fire, and mines.

The enemy launched a large-scale assault against the vitally important routes on the Huong and Cua Viet Rivers in northern I Corps. The intensity of these continuing attacks became so great that on 20 February 1968, General Abrams, the deputy commander of the forward headquarters of the Military Assistance Command, requested that a naval task force be organized to coordinate the protection of the watercraft using the rivers to resupply Hue and Dong Ha.

In rapid response to this request, Rear Admiral Kenneth L. Veth, Commander of Naval Forces, Vietnam, organized Task Force CLEARWATER whose headquarters was operational at Tan My on 24 February. Captain Gerald W. Smith, U.S. Navy, was designated the task force commander and was placed under the operational control of the commanding general of the III Marine Amphibious Force. The initial forces assigned to the Task Force CLEARWATER

LANDING CRAFT, MEDIUM

included river patrol boats of naval Task Force 116, helicopter gun ships, attack aircraft, artillery, and ground security troops. The task force concentrated on organizing and protecting shipping on the Huong River between Tan My and Hue and on the Cua Viet River between the port at Cua Viet and the base at Dong Ha.

Even after the establishment of Task Force CLEARWATER, enemy forces continued to harass and ambush utility craft as they moved their supplies along the river. At the end of February the enemy threat was still impressive, but it was apparent that many of the planned attacks were thwarted by the protective procedures practiced by Task Force CLEARWATER.

Captain Smith divided Task Force CLEARWATER into the Hue River security group and the Dong Ha River security group. On 2 March, in recognition of the enlarged importance that the northern Dong Ha River group was assuming, Captain Smith moved his headquarters from Tan My to Cua Viet. The original tactics used by the task force called for the operation of convoys protected by patrol boats and helicopter gun ships with security forces used to react in cases of ambush. The Hue River security group received convoys which were formed at Tan My while the Dong Ha Security group received them from Cua Viet. When formed, the convoys consisted of an escort unit and a movement unit, both under the command of a designated convoy commander. The escort unit was to provide for the uninterrupted transit of the movement unit by employing mine countermeasures and direct fire support and by co-ordinating aircraft, artillery, and gun fire support.

The nature of Task Force CLEARWATER operations can be understood from this log dated 26 February 1968:

1. Today's convoy of 3 LCU's, 2 Bladderboats and LCM–8 escorted by 4 PBRs, 1 LCM–8 and 4 VNN junks. The convoy departed Tan My for Hue at 0830H. Preplanned artillery missions were fired into known ambush sites as the convoy came under B–40/41 attack . . . Fire was suppressed by combined fire of gunships, PBRs and convoy craft. LCU 1574 received one B–40/41 round in the port side of coxswain flat wounding 2 USA. When the convoy cleared the ambush site the area was taken under fire by 81mm mortar.
2. When the convoy arrived at Hue at 1120H tank trucks and cargo trucks were available and offloading commenced immediately.
3. At 1300H convoy of LCUs, 3 empty Bladderboats, and 1 LCM–8 departed Hue for Tan My . . . gunships provided continual harassment fire into previous ambush sites as convoy passed. At 1310 the last LCM in the convoy came under R/R fire but the round fell short. Suppressing fire was immediate from PBRs and gunships. . . . The remainder of the transit was without incident. . . .

Not all convoys were as fortunate. On the following day, 27 February, a utility landing craft bearing explosives was hit with a B–40 rocket, and the craft exploded with such force that the nearest escort river patrol boat was also disabled.

As the security situation along the waterways gradually improved, convoying was discontinued, first on the Huong River and then on the Cua Viet. The emphasis was shifted to sweeps by river patrol boats and mine clearing operations. In early March, the task force took the offensive and began using river patrol boats and armored troop carriers for troop insertions and gun fire support. Since the enemy's ability to conduct ambushes was limited by the presence of more friendly forces along the bank, he attempted to compensate by the increased use of mines. To hinder the enemy night emplacement of mines, patrols on the Cua Viet River often began during the hours of darkness.

CHAPTER IV

U.S. Response to the *TET* Offensive

One of the commander's most powerful tools in influencing the outcome of any action is his personal presence at a critical time and place. As the intentions of the enemy in northern I Corps came into sharper focus, General Westmoreland on 25 January directed that a Military Assistance Command, Vietnam, Forward Command Post, be set up in the I Corps Tactical Zone. This move provided the commander with a field headquarters to observe, direct, and if necessary, control operations in the threatened northern provinces. General Creighton W. Abrams, designated Commander, U.S. Military Assistance Command Vietnam Forward, provided the requisite command presence with his arrival at the new post on 13 February 1968. Major General Willard Pearson, Assistant Chief of Staff for Operations, was designated Deputy Commander and Chief of Staff of the forward command post. About half the personnel required to staff the organization were selected from Headquarters, U.S. Army, Vietnam; 7th U.S. Air Force; and Naval Forces, Vietnam. Additional personnel came from Headquarters, Military Assistance Command, itself and from other field agencies.

The area of primary interest for the forward command post was the threatened northern provinces of Quang Tri and Thua Thien. The forward command post was established at Phu Bai near Hue. The 3d Marine Division rear echelon relocated from this site north to Dong Ha, and thus a minimum of preparation was required before the command post could move in.

Lieutenant Colonel Wallace J. Gross, deputy headquarters commandant of the forward command post, arrived at Phu Bai on 28 January to plan for the arrival of the headquarters. Colonel Gross was the first member of the new command to arrive. The next day a contingent of 17 officers and 14 enlisted men, led by Brigadier General Salve H. Matheson, operations officer for the forward post, arrived at Phu Bai. General Matheson remained in charge of the advance party until the command group arrived. The group was augmented by a communications element of the 459th Signal Battalion, 1st Signal Brigade, which arrived on 28 and 29 January. At 2045, on 29 January, communications were established between Military Assistance Command at Tan Son Nhut near Saigon and the forward command post at Phu Bai.

On 30 January, the staff of the forward command post began functioning from Room 2H03 in the Military Assistance Command headquarters at Tan Son Nhut. The staff determined what additional personnel and equipment would be required to operate the forward command post, requested the principal appointments to fill these requirements, and phased personnel, supplies, and equipment into the field headquarters at Phu Bai. By 2 February, staff personnel and a headquarters support unit reported to Phu Bai. General Abrams arrived at the Military Assistance command post on 13 February and two days later assumed operational control of the 1st Cavalry Division and all other U.S. Army forces deploying to the two northern provinces. The accomplishment of organizing, activating, staffing, and deploying such a headquarters during a period of intense enemy activity was a tribute to the ability of the organizing staff.

At the command post the following priorities were promptly established: to reduce the siege of Hue, to open lines of communications and stockpile needed supplies for future operations, to receive U.S. Army reinforcements being deployed into the northern provinces from other corps, and to initiate planning for the relief of the Khe Sanh combat base.

In the ensuing weeks the equivalent of one U.S. Army corps moved into the "heart of Marine land" and came under the operational control of the Military Assistance Command forward post. Although General Abrams was best recognized in Army circles as a tough soldier with a solid background in logistics, as the commander of the forward post he proved his other talents as a diplomat and statesman of the first rank. Enroute to his new headquarters from Saigon he visited the headquarters of the III Marine Amphibious Force and while there he and General Cushman, the Marine commander, decided the fight would be against the enemy and not an interservice one. Considering the crucial nature of the situation prevailing at the time, a surprising degree of harmony keynoted Army and Marine operations during the following months of intensive fighting.

As a modus operandi, the dispatch of messages by the forward Military Assistance Command to the commanding general of the III Marine Amphibious Force, recommended operational and logistical actions to improve the combat capabilities of forces in northern I Corps. Information copies of such messages went to the commander of the Military Assistance Command in Saigon. One example of this procedure took place during the siege of Hue and involved artillery support. General Abrams dispatched a message to the commanding general of the III Marine Amphibious Force, with an information copy to Saigon, recommending that one battery of 8-inch howitzers be deployed from southern I Corps where enemy activity had subsided to the Phu Bai area to provide heavy artillery needed to breach the walls around the Hue Citadel. The requested battery was immediately relieved of its current mission and flown to Phu Bai in support of the operation.

The day General Abrams arrived at Phu Bai, 13 February, the decision was made to deploy the understrength 101st Airborne Division into the area of operation of the forward command post. The airborne division was minus a brigade which remained in III Corps and a battalion task force operating in II Corps. Within weeks the 3d Brigade, 82d Airborne Division, flew in from Fort Bragg, North Carolina, and came under control of the 101st Airborne Division. Another major unit programed into I Corps was the 27th U.S. Marine Corps Regimental Landing Team airlifted from California which arrived 23 February.

Planning for the Relief of Khe Sanh

As the immediate *Tet* emergency became less critical, the Military Assistance Command, Vietnam, Forward Command Post began to plan for the relief of Khe Sanh. This planning continued as the siege of Hue was reduced, as U.S. Army reinforcements were deployed into the area, and as lines of communication were opened and stockpiles reconstituted. When it became apparent that the logistical-over-the-shore (LOTS) supply facility could comfortably discharge over 1,000 tons a day, 1 April was set as D-day for the relief of Khe Sanh.

Before the end of February a concept for the relief of Khe Sanh was presented by the forward command post staff to the recently appointed deputy commander, General William B. Rosson, and subsequently to General Abrams and General Cushman. It was refined and used as a basis for concurrent planning by the major subordinate commands of the Military Assistance Command forward post.

On 10 March 1968 the Military Assistance Command, Vietnam, Forward Command Post was redesignated Provisional Corps, Vietnam. The following press release dated 8 March outlines the command relationships of the new headquarters:

General William C. Westmoreland, Commander of the U.S. Military Assistance Command, Vietnam, announced today the formation of a new headquarters to assist in the command and control of U.S. units in the northern part of the First Corps Tactical Zone.
The new headquarters will be commanded by Army Lieutenant

General William B. Rosson and will be designated as Provisional Corps, Vietnam. It will no doubt be more widely known to Military personnel by its short title of "Prov Corps, V."

The headquarters staff will consist mainly of Army and Marine Corps personnel, though it also will contain some Navy and Air Force officers. The new headquarters will exercise operational control of U.S. military ground units in the northern provinces of Quang Tri and Thua Thien. The Provisional Corps will be subordinate to Marine Lieutenant General Robert E. Cushman, Commanding General of the Third Marine Amphibious Force in Da Nang, who has several other senior tactical units reporting to him. It will serve as a tactical echelon between General Cushman and the Commanders of the U.S. Army and Marine Divisions in the northern area. General Cushman's area of responsibilities will remain unchanged.

General Rosson will also have coordinating functions with the highly regarded First Vietnamese Division which is deployed in the area.

Most of the personnel in the new headquarters will come from the MACV Forward Headquarters which was established in the area several weeks ago under command of General Creighton W. Abrams. General Abrams, who is General Westmoreland's deputy, has effected coordination among the Army, Navy, Marine and Air Force units in the area. Since his assigned task is virtually complete, he will now return to his normal duties in Saigon and the forward headquarters will cease to exist.

At 1201 hours, 10 March 1968, Provisional Corps, Vietnam, became operational at Phu Bai under command of Lieutenant General Rosson. The corps assumed operational control of two Army and one Marine Corps divisions and Task Force CLEARWATER, together with other combat and service support units. Major General Willard Pearson remained as the deputy commander and chief of staff, and Brigadier General Lawrence H. Caruthers assumed command of the artillery of Provisional Corps, Vietnam. Subsequently, Major General Raymond G. Davis, U.S. Marine Corps, became the deputy commander of Provisional Corps, Vietnam.

The day he assumed command, General Rosson briefed General Westmoreland on the planned operations for the corps. Three distinct operational target areas were presented: the elimination of enemy forces in the Con Thien–Gio Linh area north of Dong Ha; the opening of Route 9 with the subsequent relief of Khe San Combat Base; and an assault into the A Shau Valley. General Westmoreland approved the operations in the Con Thien–Gio Linh area to be followed immediately by the Khe Sanh operation. The A Shau operation was to be conducted as a reconnaissance-in-force operation at a later date.

The corps planned to begin the Con Thien–Gio Linh operation first and to follow it immediately, on or about 1 April, with the Khe Sanh operation. The outline for the Khe Sanh plan provided that the 1st Cavalry Division would conduct air assaults while the 1st Marine Regiment and Vietnamese Army Task Force would execute an overland attack. At the same time, Route 547 from Hue to the A Shau Valley would be interdicted by air strikes and the valley itself subjected to additional air reconnaissance in order to locate targets for air and artillery strikes. General Westmoreland approved these plans. The Army's 1st Cavalry Division under the command of Major General John J. Tolson, III, was assigned overall operational responsibility for the relief of Khe Sanh. The offensive plan was called Operation PEGASUS after the winged horse of Greek mythology.

On 15 March, General Rosson's headquarters requested the participation of a Vietnamese Army task force in the Khe Sanh operation. This step was recommended not only for sound military reasons, but also because it was considered desirable to have major Vietnamese troops participate in the relief of Khe Sanh. A task force of three airborne battalions was made available on 28 March.

On 16 March, a logistical planning group was formed at the headquarters of the Provisional Corps to determine requirements for the offensive. The three divisions under the Provisional Corps, the 101st Airborne, the 1st Air Cavalry, and the 3d Marine were directed to send representatives, and the III Marine Amphibious Force was requested to send a representative to speak for the Da Nang Support Command, Navy Support Activity, Da Nang, and the Fleet Logistic Command.

To reduce the time required for helicopters to transfer supplies from airfields to troop field positions, airfields had to be as close as possible to operational areas. The less time required per trip, the fewer helicopters would be required. Accordingly, the planning group concluded that PEGASUS should receive logistical support from a base operated by the U.S. Army Support Command near Ca Lu. To insure continuous support, the base was to be prestocked before 1 April. To meet this goal, the logistical base was established 21 March and the next day the first of daily convoys from Dong Ha made its supply run to Ca Lu.

At Ca Lu engineers began to construct an area for an ammunition storage facility, bunkers, helicopter revetments, a road network for the supply base, fields of fire around the perimeter to improve security, and an area for petroleum, oil, and lubricants; construction of the airstrip began at the same time.

Communications planning for Operation PEGASUS indicated a need to considerably upgrade the established system. The terrain in the operational area and distances over which the signals must travel dictated that a signal hill be established. The 1st Cavalry

Division prepared and secured the complex, while the United States Army, Vietnam, and the III Marine Amphibious Force provided the needed equipment. This feat was accomplished with signal resources not under the control of the headquarters of the Provisional Corps, Vietnam. When the Military Assistance Command, Vietnam, Forward Command Post had been established, it had made do with signal support provided by other units. During February 1968, the 459th Signal Battalion had grown to support the command posts needs. When the Provisional Corps was activated, this function continued and expanded. The 459th Signal Battalion, redesignated the 63d Signal Battalion, had then assumed direct support of the headquarters of the Provisional Corps in addition to its other missions. To facilitate this change, the battalion was removed from the operational control of the 21st Signal Group at Nha Trang and instructed to answer directly to the U.S. Army's 1st Signal Brigade.

Headquarters, U.S. Army, Vietnam, directed the Provisional Corps signal officer to function as its area communications co-ordinator and representative for the northern two provinces of I Corps. This arrangement gave the Provisional Corps signal officer access to more communications support than normally available to a corps headquarters. Although somewhat unorthodox, the system proved highly efficient in actual practice.

The improvement of communications systems had earlier been extended into Khe Sanh itself. The deputy commanding general of U.S. Army, Vietnam, directed the 1st Signal Brigade to establish a tactical tropospheric scatter system from Khe Sanh. The system provided teletypewriter and voice circuits of the highest quality and the 1st Signal Brigade kept the system in service throughout the campaign.

Single Manager for Air Concept

On 8 March 1968 General Westmoreland designated his deputy for air operations, General William W. Momyer, U.S. Air Force, as the single manager for control of tactical air resources in South Vietnam to include all U.S. Marine fixed-wing strike and reconnaissance aircraft. This action was taken as a result of the buildup of Army forces in I Corps, the corresponding concentration of tactical air sorties in support of these forces, and an overriding requirement to maintain maximum flexibility in allocating air resources during the particularly critical period following the Communist *Tet* offensive.

A look at the statistics on the air operations supporting the

ground forces at Khe Sanh from mid-January until the end of March
1968 pointed out the need for a single focal point in co-ordinating
the air effort. During this period there were nearly 10,000 Air Force
fighter strikes, over 5,000 Navy and 7,000 Marine strikes, and over
2,500 B–52 strikes, for a total of more than 24,500 air strikes.

General Westmoreland's decision ran directly counter to Marine
doctrine and tradition and was not welcomed by the III Marine
Amphibious Force. The commanding general of the force opposed
the single manager concept on the grounds that it was neither
doctrinally nor functionally suited to his requirements. However, as
the situation in I Corps changed, the concept was implemented on
10 March 1968 as approved by the Pacific commander in chief. The
system actually became effective about 1 April 1968.

Integrated with the tactical air operation was the air resupply
of troops at Khe Sanh. The following table shows the number of
personnel and tons of supplies airlifted into Khe Sanh in March
1968.

Date	Short Tons	Personnel
3 March	193	30
4 March	184	73
8 March	219	21
9 March	201	36
10 March	195	116
16 March	172	
17 March	243	
20 March	292+448 barrels POL	
21 March	247+554 barrels POL	
23 March	232	
24 March	233	
25 March	149	
26 March	149	
27 March	161	
28 March	148.6	
29 March	235	
30 March	240	

Clearly the close air support and air resupply by the U.S. Air
Force and Marine Corps as well as helicopter supply operations by
the U.S. Army played a major role in the defeat of the North Vietnamese Army during the Khe Sanh operation.

CHAPTER V

Khe Sanh and PEGASUS

The base at Khe Sanh remained relatively quiet throughout the first week of the enemy *Tet* offensive, but the lull ended with a heavy ground attack on the morning of 5 February. The enemy penetrated the perimeter of the position on Hill 861A, and the resulting hand-to-hand combat drove the enemy back. A second attempt to overrun the position was less successful than the first. Elsewhere the North Vietnamese were more successful when, on 7 February, they struck at the Special Forces camp at Lang Vei.

The Lang Vei Special Forces Camp was located astride Route 9 some nine kilometers west of Khe Sanh Village. Beginning about 1800 on 6 February, the camp was subjected to an unusually intense mortar and artillery barrage. The defenders immediately responded with counter fire from the camp and requested supporting fire from the Khe Sanh Combat Base.

The enemy ground attack began about midnight on the morning of 7 February. The initial force to reach the protective wire around the perimeter included two of the approximately twelve Russian manufactured PT–76 amphibious tanks. The two armored vehicles were sighted in the outer wire on the southern side of the camp, taken under fire, and knocked out. (*Map 10*)

The armor defeating weapons in the camp consisted of two 106-mm. recoilless rifles, a few 57-mm. recoilless rifles, and 100 light antitank weapons known as LAW'S. The LAW is designed to be fired once and discarded. These special weapons had been provided to the camp shortly before the attack as a result of intelligence reports which indicated that an attack was imminent and that armored vehicles would most likely be involved. Because of the newness of the weapons, few of the indigenous personnel and only half of the Americans had had the opportunity to fire the weapon before the attack. One survivor reported that several LAW'S failed to fire. This may have been due to lack of training or to improper storage.

Additional tanks moved around the destroyed vehicles and overran the company manning the southern sector. The friendly troops pulled back, but continued fighting. They fought the tanks with small arms, machine guns, hand grenades, and antitank weap-

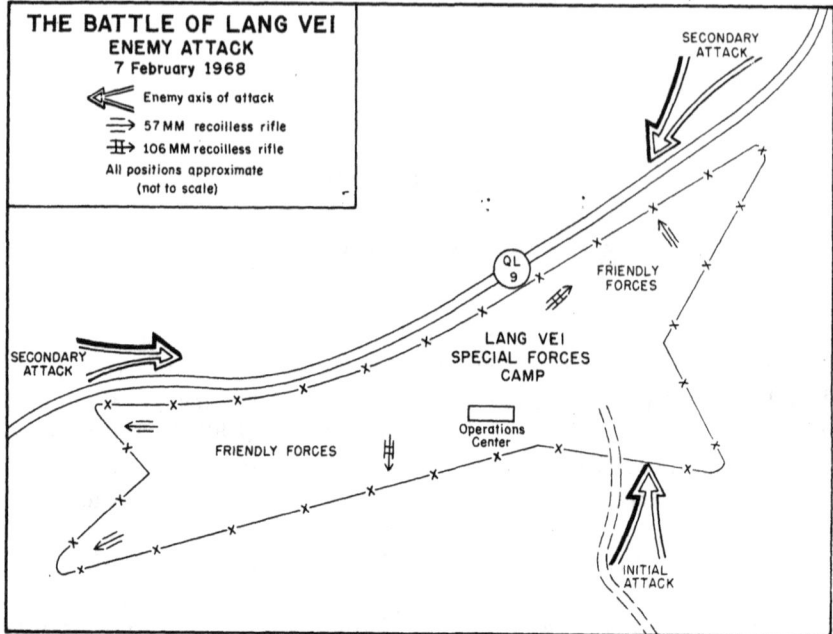

THE BATTLE OF LANG VEI
ENEMY ATTACK
7 February 1968

Enemy axis of attack
57 MM recoilless rifle
106 MM recoilless rifle
All positions approximate
(not to scale)

SECONDARY ATTACK

QL 9

FRIENDLY FORCES

LANG VEI SPECIAL FORCES CAMP

SECONDARY ATTACK

Operations Center

FRIENDLY FORCES

INITIAL ATTACK

MAP 10

ons. As the attack continued, the defenders were forced to continue their withdrawal from the forward positions. They re-formed in pockets and continued to resist and fire at the enemy troops and tanks as they moved through the camp. As the enemy soldiers advanced, they used explosive charges to demolish the fortifications within the camp. The enemy tanks used their 76-mm. main guns against the combat positions and tactical operations center in the camp.

As the battle continued, air strikes were called in. When day broke over the battlefield, the defenders located in the operations center called for and received air support to assist them in breaking out of the still surrounded position. Their escape was aided by a rescue force that had returned to the camp to help extract survivors. By day's end the camp had been evacuated and all surviving personnel extracted.

As the Lang Vei battle progressed, the Marines were requested to implement their contingency plan to reinforce the Special Forces camp. However, because of the fear that this attack was but a part of an all-out general attack in the area, Lang Vei was not reinforced. By noon on the 7th, General Westmoreland was being briefed on the need to evacuate the survivors. Also at the meeting were General Cushman and General Tompkins. General Westmoreland directed that aircraft be made available to support the reaction force, and that afternoon the extraction took place.

When 7 February came to an end, the Lang Vei Camp was empty. Almost half of the 500 defenders were dead or missing. The survivors left behind them seven destroyed enemy tanks and at least as many enemy casualties as they themselves had suffered. The enemy attack stopped at the camp. It did not continue east toward Khe Sanh.

At Khe Sanh the marines were monitoring the battle at Lang Vei. After the seriously wounded had been evacuated by helicopter, the remaining survivors and many refugees moved east on foot. On the morning of 8 February some 3,000 refugees, including the Lang Vei survivors and Laotian 33d Battalion troops who had withdrawn from their attacked position on 23 January, appeared at the front gate of the Khe Sanh perimeter. At first denied admittance, the people were later searched and permitted to enter. Most were soon evacuated out of the area with the Laotians being returned to their own country.

At 0420, 8 February, a reinforced enemy battalion assaulted a platoon position of the 9th Marine Regiment. The marines were forced back from that portion of their perimeter which bore the brunt of the assault, but maintained control of most of the position. A company-sized counterattack at mid-morning restored the position, but the Marine commander at Khe Sanh decided to evacuate that platoon position because of its exposed location.

Enemy pressure on the Khe Sanh Combat Base continued during the following two weeks but not in the form of any major ground attacks. Probes, minor clashes, and sniping incidents occurred daily although the main enemy interest appeared to be the consolidation of his position and preparation for an all-out effort. In attempts to deter these preparations by artillery and air strikes, the marines were themselves hindered by the weather.

During this period Khe Sanh and its surrounding outposts continued to be supplied almost entirely by air. Marine and Air Force cargo aircraft made numerous daily runs to keep the base provisioned, to bring in replacement troops, and to take out wounded. The pilots had to brave both poor weather and intense enemy antiaircraft fire to accomplish these tasks.

On 10 February, a Marine C–130, loaded with fuel containers, was laced with bullets just before touching down on the runway. The aircraft was lost along with some of the passengers and crew. This incident caused major revisions in the off-loading procedure. As a result of this loss and the damage inflicted on other aircraft while on the ground, landings of the large C–130 type aircraft were suspended at Khe Sanh on 23 February.

Operation NIAGARA II continued throughout this period. This intensive air interdiction campaign continued to provide excellent results. The high volume reconnaissance missions, added to other intelligence sources, recommended an average of at least 150 targets per day. On 15 February, one of the most lucrative targets, an ammunition storage area, was pinpointed 19 kilometers south southwest of Khe Sanh in the Co Roc Mountain region. Flight after flight of strike aircraft were directed into the area throughout a 24-hour period. Many secondary explosions and fires revealed additional stockpiles which were in turn attacked. In all, it proved to be a good day's work resulting in over 1,000 secondary explosions and fires, some of which continued two and one-half hours after a series of strikes had been completed.

Air operations on the logistical side also progressed. Following the termination of C–130 aircraft landings, the Air Force introduced a new procedure to continue supplying the main Khe Sanh base. Known as the Low Altitude Parachute Extraction System or LAPES, this self-contained method of delivery had been put to good use while the air strip was being repaired in late 1967. The name of the system accurately described the technique. As the aircraft came in low over the airstrip, the pilot opened the tail gate and released a reefed cargo parachute which was connected to the pallet mounted cargo in the aircraft. When the pilot electrically cut the reefing line, it caused the parachute to fully deploy and inflate. The parachute then jerked the pallets out of the aircraft over the roller system mounted on the aircraft floor. After a five- to ten-foot drop, the cargo skidded to a halt on the runway. Experienced pilots could consistently leave their loads in a 25-meter square.

A second technique was also used to deliver cargo by aircraft without actually landing. This method, known as the Ground Proximity Extraction System or GPES, was used less frequently than the low altitude system. In the GPES delivery, as the C–130 aircraft came in low over the airstrip, the pilot would try to snag an arresting line on the ground similar to the line a navy pilot uses in landing on an aircraft carrier. The ground line then jerked the cargo from the opened rear of the aircraft.

About 65 deliveries using the low altitude and ground proximity systems were made before Khe Sanh was relieved and resupply effected by way of Route 9. By far, the majority of the supplies for the base were delivered by parachute because weather was too poor to permit the visual flying required for the two extraction type systems.

Another aspect of the air operations was the last leg of the re-supply system in which helicopters picked up supplies at Dong Ha and carried them to the outposts on the surrounding hills. They faced the same problems as did the fixed-wing pilots, but to a greater degree. The low-flying helicopter pilots were more vulner-able than their higher flying, faster fellow aviators. Because of the additional exposure, helicopters soon were escorted by strike air-craft to provide suppressive fire as they dropped off supplies and picked up troops.

Helicopters were greatly affected by the weather. When the heli-copters were grounded, life became hard on the marines in the out-posts. One period of weather when the helicopters could not fly persisted for nine days and created such a water shortage that one small position was authorized to conduct a two-hour march to ob-tain water from the nearest stream. The patrol surprised a group of enemy soldiers and eliminated many of them.

Fighting on the ground in Operation SCOTLAND, a Marine designation, continued through the end of February. The last day of the month, 29 February, General Tompkins and Colonel Lownds pieced together the relevant facts to reason that a big enemy push was imminent. Each day brought better weather and longer flying hours. Numerous intelligence reports pointed to a massing of North Vietnamese units at three points around the main base. Although the enemy had failed to gain control of the hill outposts, he could not afford to let the weather improve much more before he acted.

During the early evening hours of 29 February, a string of sen-sors indicated a major movement of troops along Route 9. The fire support control center at the base directed all available assets against the area. The firepower was massive. Artillery, radar-guided fighter bombers, and minor and major B–52 strikes pounded the enemy's route of march.

A battalion of the 304th North Vietnamese Army Divison made the first strike at 2130 on 29 February. The 37th Vietnamese Army Ranger Battalion received the brunt of the initial assault, and all available supporting fire was given the rangers. Hit with this con-centrated firepower, the enemy was unable to breach the outer defenses. His second attempt two hours later met a similar fate. So did the third at 0315 on 1 March. The supporting fires had pre-vented the assault waves from gaining momentum.

Although the enemy continued to harass the base, to probe the weakness along the perimeter, and to shell it from a distance, he had changed his basic tactics. He assumed a less aggressive posture and began waiting for the Marine patrols to come to him. But this did not help him either. As time passed and the weather improved, indications by mid-March were that major North Vietnamese Army units were leaving the area around Khe Sanh.

The Marine's last significant clash during Operation SCOTLAND took place on 30 March when a company, moving under a closely co-ordinated artillery support package, swept 850 meters south of the Khe Sanh perimeter and assaulted a heavily fortified enemy position. Surprise was with the attackers, however, and the marines drove the enemy out of his positions, destroyed the fortifications, and returned to their base.

Planning for Pegasus

The next day at 0800, SCOTLAND was officially ended. At that time, the operational control of the 26th Marine Regiment at Khe Sanh passed to the 1st Cavalry Division (Airmobile) which initiated Operation PEGASUS. The details of this operation are covered in Chapter V.

Elsewhere in northern I Corps Tactical Zone, it became apparent during late March that the enemy was continuing to build his base areas along Route 547 and had constructed an alternate route, 547A, from the A Shau Valley east towards Hue. These routes provided the enemy with a major artery for the movement of troops, supplies, and equipment out of the valley and into the denser jungle area between the valley and Hue. Reconnaissance of the area revealed a sophisticated communications system using wire lines and the presence of heavy automatic and antiaircraft weapons. Numerous caches of weapons, ammunition, and other equipment had been located by elements of the 101st Airborne Division operating along Route 547 and 547A west of Hue. These caches indicated the presence of 37-mm. antiaircraft cannons and tracked vehicles, probably tanks, in the area. General Westmoreland, after his 17 March visit to Provisional Corps, Vietnam, directed B–52 tactical airstrikes to interdict Route 547 and 547A.

Final preparations were being made for relieving the siege of Khe Sanh by the reinforced 1st Cavalry Division. On 22 March General Rosson held a meeting with division commanders at Camp Evans, 15 kilometers southeast of Quang Tri City and formulated plans for the relief of 1st Cavalry Division elements from their area of operation along the coastal areas of Quang Tri Province by units of the 101st Airborne Division. To insure that a sufficient force would be available to offset a new enemy threat at Hue, General Rosson requested that the Vietnamese Marine Task Force be retained at Hue. If the force could not be retained, he requested that a fourth Vietnamese Airborne Battalion and U.S. forces be made available for employment in the Hue area. General Cushman forwarded General Rosson's report to General Westmoreland with a recommendation that the airborne task force be raised to four battalions for the Con Thien–Gio Linh operation. The Con Thien operation was envisioned as a deception plan for Operation PEGASUS. This operation would also place the airborne task force closer to the ultimate zone of action in the Khe Sanh Operation.

General Rosson, Captain Smith, the commanding officer of Task Force CLEARWATER, and the Commander of the Naval Support Activity in Da Nang met at the III Marine Amphibious Force headquarters with General Cushman to discuss the deception plan and to determine the details of its implementation and its effect on logistical support in northern I Corps Tactical Zone.

Operation Orders

The Third Marine Division issued its operation order on 25 March to cover both the Con Thien–Gio Linh operation, which would be executed in conjunction with U.S. Army elements and the 1st Vietnamese Division, and Operation PEGASUS. The 4th Marine Regiment was to secure Route 9 and provide convoy security in its area. The 9th Marine Regiment was to provide security for Route 9 in its sector. The 12th Marine Regiment was instructed to support the attack of the 1st Cavalry Division within its artillery capabilities.

As the emeny activity around Khe Sanh tapered off, it appeared that Operation PEGASUS might go much quicker than originally anticipated. If true, this would relieve elements of the 1st Cavalry Division for earlier commitment to attacks in the A Shau Valley area. General Westmoreland expressed the view that Operation PEGASUS was to exact the maximum destruction of enemy forces and facilities, and its duration would therefore have to depend on the tactical situation as it developed. General Cushman and General Rosson assured General Westmoreland that all preparations for Operation PEGASUS would be ready for the planned 1 April attack. General Westmoreland also approved the concept for a later operation in the A Shau Valley presented by the III Marine Amphibious Force. Thus, the logistical planning for the operation into the A Shau Valley was conducted concurrently with logistical support for PEGASUS and it was envisioned that the second operation would continue as a smooth transition from the first.

Provisional Corps, Vietnam, Operation Plan I–68 was redesignated Operation Order I–68 with D-day, H-hour, established as 01001 April. General Tompkins, Commanding General, 3d Marine Division, ordered the execution of a deception operation with D-day,

H-hour, established as 0600 on 30 March. The U.S. elements participating in the combined operation were designated Task Force KILO and the Vietnamese Army portion of the operation designated LAM SON 203. The deception operation envisioned a task force attacking northeast from Dong Ha toward the demilitarized zone.

As the final co-ordination was being accomplished to insure all units were ready for the pending operation, some elements were already at work. In addition to the U.S. Air Force actions in preparation for the operation, the 1st Squadron, 9th Cavalry of the 1st Cavalry Division, was directing strikes to eliminate antiaircraft positions in the area before the airmobile division committed the bulk of its helicopters. Heavy U.S. Air Force strikes had stripped away much of the concealment needed by the enemy. With the addition of the reconnaissance squadron of the 1st Cavalry Division, the effectiveness of artillery and air strikes directed against the enemy antiaircraft positions was almost total. As the final hours of March ticked away, the Free World Forces awaited the signal to strike.

CHAPTER VI

The Free World Counteroffensive

Opening Operations

At 0600, 30 March, U.S. Army, Marine, and Vietnamese Army forces initiated their planned deception operation northeast of Dong Ha. The U.S. element consisted of the 3d Squadron, 5th Cavalry; Company C, 2d Battalion, 34th Armor; Company A, 1st Battalion, 502d Airborne, 101st Airborne Division; and 2d Battalion, 4th Marine Regiment; all controlled by the 3d Marine Division. The Vietnamese Army element consisted of the 1st Battalion, 2d Infantry, and the 3d Battalion, 1st Infantry, under the control of the 1st Vietnamese Army Infantry Division. The maneuver elements attacked generally north toward the demilitarized zone along the coastal plains near Gio Linh. All units reached their objectives that afternoon. Following only light action, the operation was terminated on the afternoon of 1 May.

The broad concept for the relief of Khe Sanh envisioned the 1st Cavalry Division attacking west from Ca Lu to seize the high ground along Highway 9 in a series of successive air mobile assaults. Concurrently the marines were to secure and repair Highway 9 leading to Khe Sanh. Under the single manager concept for air, intensive close air support was to assist the attacks, together with massive B-52 strikes prior to and during the assault. Major units reinforcing the 1st Cavalry Division were the 1st Marine Regiment with three battalions and an airborne task force of three battalions, plus the supporting combat and service units. (Chart 3)

Operation PEGASUS began at 0700 on 1 April with U.S. Army, U.S. Marine, and Vietnamese forces moving out from Ca Lu along Highway 9 toward the Khe Sanh Combat Base. The 1st Cavalry Division attacked with a combination of air and ground assaults to clear and secure the road and remove the enemy from the area of operation. During the morning hours, the two lead Marine battalions moved out according to plan, pushing west from Ca Lu. Delayed by weather, it was not until 1300 that the initial waves of 1st Cavalry Division helicopters placed men of the 3d Brigade of the Cavalry on a series of landing zones as close as five miles to Khe Sanh. (Map 11)

CHART 3—1ST AIR CAVALRY DIVISION ORGANIZATION FOR OPERATION PEGASUS

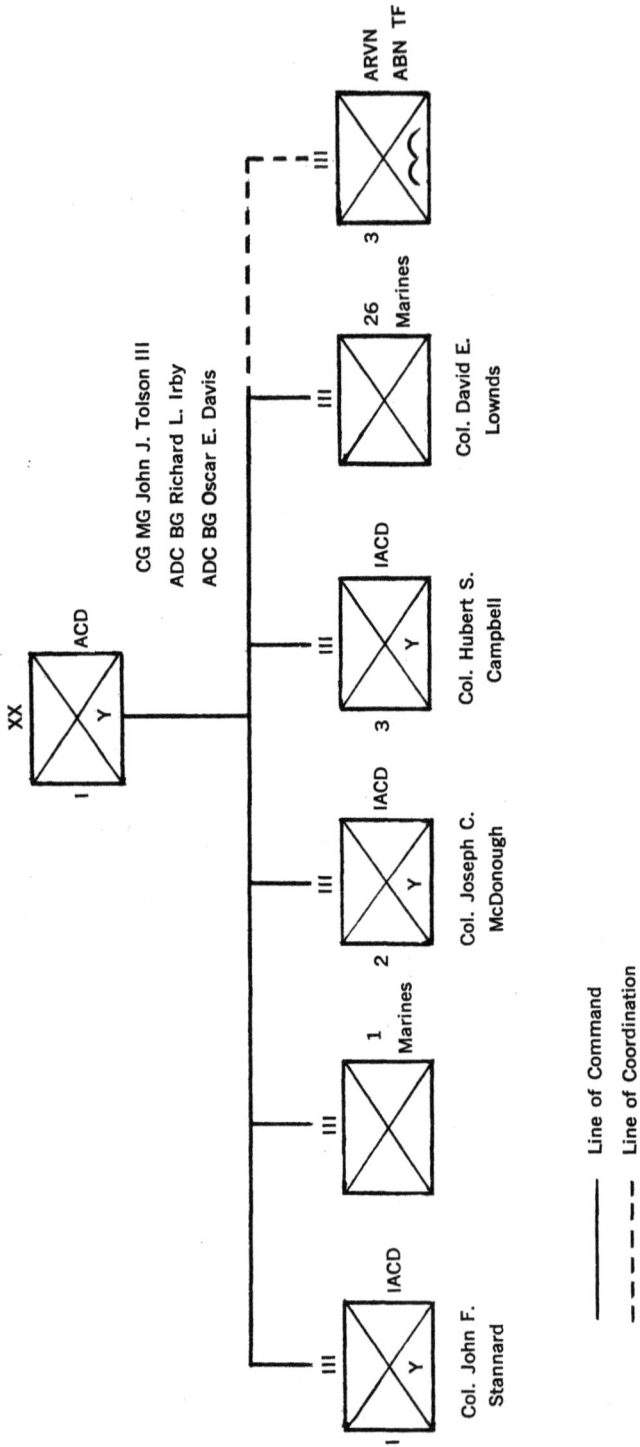

XX ACD
Y

CG MG John J. Tolson III
ADC BG Richard L. Irby
ADC BG Oscar E. Davis

IACD
Y
Col. John F. Stannard

1 Marines

2 IACD
Y
Col. Joseph C. McDonough

3 IACD
Y
Col. Hubert S. Campbell

26 Marines
Col. David E. Lownds

3 ARVN ABN TF

———— Line of Command
- - - - Line of Coordination

MAJOR MANEUVER ELEMENTS AND COMMANDERS

THE 1ST CAVALRY DIVISION DISEMBARKS *from UH – 1B for a mission.*

The 2d Battalion, 1st Marines, advanced westward on the north side of Route 9 while the 2d Battalion, 3d Marines, advanced on the south side of the road. As the Marines progressed and cleared Route 9 and the nearby terrain of enemy troops, engineer companies began repairing the road. They cleared one and a half kilometers of road and constructed four by-passes the first day. Throughout the operational area, the Americans spent a quiet night in rapidly prepared defensive positions.

Although Operation NIAGARA had been terminated with the beginning of PEGASUS, air support continued. The first day of the operation, eight B–52 raids were flown to assist the ground forces. Four of the missions were in the vicinity of Khe Sanh. Poor weather in the early daylight hours limited tactical fighter support to 66 sorties. Eight U.S. Air Force C–130 and four C–123 cargo aircraft delivered 115 tons the first day and 24 helicopter missions boosted the sum to just under 150 tons. An additional 44 personnel joined the combat base by way of C–123 aircraft, which were still permitted to land on the strip.

On 2 April operations began at 0655 with two Marine battalions resuming their advance along either side of Route 9 toward Khe Sanh. Contact with the enemy was minimal. The 2d Battalion, 7th Cavalry, began an air assault at 1300. The late starting time was

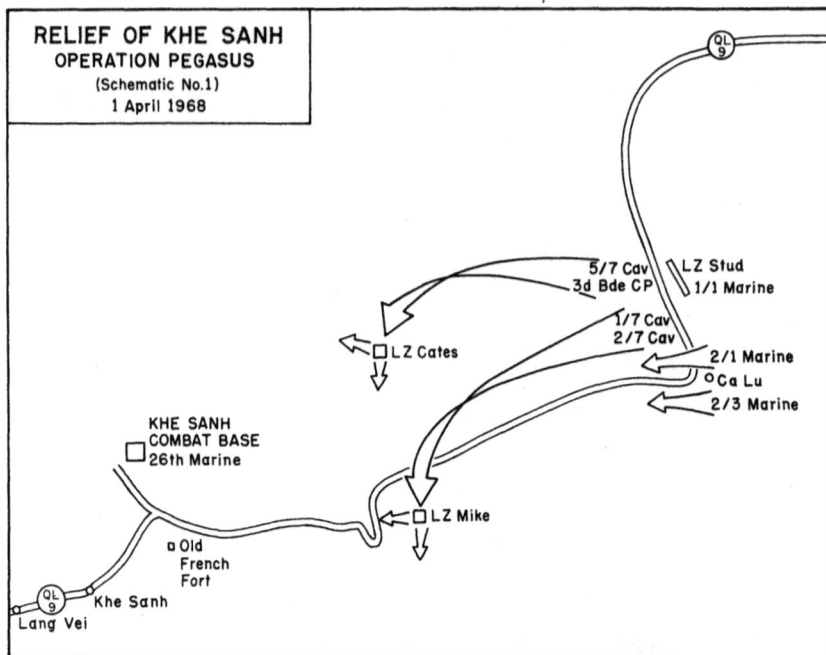

RELIEF OF KHE SANH
OPERATION PEGASUS
(Schematic No.1)
1 April 1968

5/7 Cav
3d Bde CP

LZ Stud
1/1 Marine

1/7 Cav
2/7 Cav

2/1 Marine
Ca Lu
2/3 Marine

LZ Cates

KHE SANH
COMBAT BASE
26th Marine

LZ Mike

Old
French
Fort

Khe Sanh
Lang Vei

MAP 11

attributed to ground fog, haze, and low hanging clouds. These unfavorable flying conditions continued throughout the operation.

The 1st Battalion, 1st Marines, remained near the air field north of Ca Lu, which had been designated Landing Zone STUD. The Marine unit retained this mission for the duration of the operation.

The Army, Navy, and Marine engineer units continued their work along Route 9. On 2 April they cleared almost three kilometers of the road and completed two bridges and two more bypasses. (*Map 12*)

The sustained air support included 36 B–52 aircraft delivering six strikes, five of which were in the immediate vicinity of Khe Sanh Combat Base. In spite of the unfavorable flying weather, 142 tactical air sorties were flown by Air Force, Navy, and Marine aircraft in support of the ground troops conducting PEGASUS. Air Force cargo aircraft dropped 91.4 tons of supplies into Khe Sanh and helicopters raised the total tonnage to 162.

On 3 April the tempo of the operation picked up somewhat. The marines continued westward along Route 9 with the engineers working furiously right on their heels. The 1st Cavalry's 3d Brigade continued operations in the vicinity of the landing zones they had occupied during the first day. The 2d Brigade of the 1st Cavalry

Division air-assaulted in the PEGASUS area of operations one day ahead of schedule with the 2d Battalion, 5th Cavalry, going into Landing Zone TOM and the 2d Battalion, 12th Cavalry, moving first to Landing Zone STUD by CH–47 helicopters, then reloading into smaller UH–1H helicopters for an air assault into Landing Zone WHARTON. The 1st Battalion, 5th Cavalry, then flew into Landing Zone WHARTON. Both landing zones received artillery and rocket fire from enemy positions during the moves, but the troops were not to be easily diverted. By the end of the day, all 2d Brigade troops and three batteries of the 1st Battalion, 77th Artillery, were in position. At that time, other artillery batteries in position included Battery C, 21st Artillery, which had followed the air assault troops into Landing Zone CATES, and B Battery, 21st Artillery, which had followed into Landing Zone MIKE on D-day. Battery A, 21st Artillery, joined the 2d Battalion, 7th Cavalry, at Landing Zone THOR on 2 April.

During the fourth day, April 4, the enemy resistance continued at a moderate level. The marines maintained their westward attack along the main supply route and the Third Brigade kept up pressure on enemy elements around the established landing zones. The 1st Battalion, 5th Cavalry, initiated an attack on an enemy battalion occupying positions in an old French fort.

On the same day, elements of the 26th Marine Regiment began their first major offensive move in weeks, attacking out of the Khe Sanh Combat Base. Preceded by extensive artillery preparation, at 0600 the 1st Battalion, 9th Marines, assaulted southeast towards their objective, Hill 471. The hill was secured by 1720 that day.

The fifth day, 5 April, opened with an enemy attack on Hill 471, which the Marines had occupied the previous afternoon. At 0515 the 7th Battalion, 66th Regiment, 304th North Vietnamese Division, charged up the hill. The fight was one of the highlights of Operation PEGASUS and was quite one-sided. Assisted by tremendous artillery and close air support, the marines cut down large numbers of the attackers while suffering few casualties themselves. (*Map 13*)

Elsewhere, except for the 1st Cavalry Division's 2d Brigade, the operation followed a routine pattern. The marines and the 2d Battalion, 7th Cavalry, maintained their westward movement, meeting moderate opposition along Route 9. The engineers had reconstructed a total of 5.5 kilometers of the road, completing four bridges and twelve by-passes.

The Marine advance along the main supply route continued through 6 April. The 2d Battalion, 7th Cavalry, maintained its drive west and met stubborn enemy resistance occasioning the heaviest fighting of the operation thus far. Following a day-long battle, the

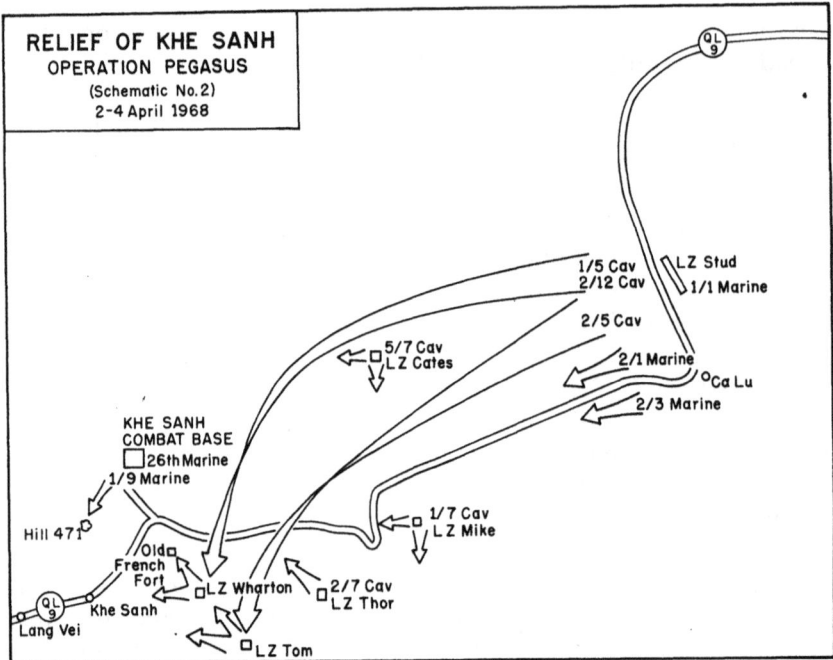

MAP 12

cavalry finally drove the enemy out of his defensive positions, capturing 121 individual and 10 crew-served weapons.

The 2d Battalion, 12th Cavalry, was airlifted from Landing
Zone TIMOTHY to Hill 471 and effected relief of the 1st Battalion,
9th Marines, at noon. The marines then opened a clearing attack to
the northwest.

Meanwhile the 1st Battalion of the 5th Cavalry was encountering
stiff resistance at an old French fort about 15 kilometers due east of
Khe Sanh. On the sixth day of Operation PEGASUS the 1st of the 5th
was extracted and the 2d Battalion of the 5th Cavalry picked up the
mission of seizing the strongly defended position. The fort finally
fell on 7 April thus eliminating the final known enemy strongpoint
between the advance cavalry troopers and Khe Sanh.

Little further significant contact was to occur during the final
days of the operation. The remainder of Operation PEGASUS was
directed at opening the main supply route and sifting through the
debris of battle. The retreating enemy continued to offer some
resistance, but without spirit.

The seventh day, 7 April, witnessed a further lessening of enemy
strength in the area of operations. Ground probes against friendly
positions continued but fewer reports were made of attacks by enemy artillery.

At 0800 on 8 April, the relief of the Khe Sanh Combat Base was

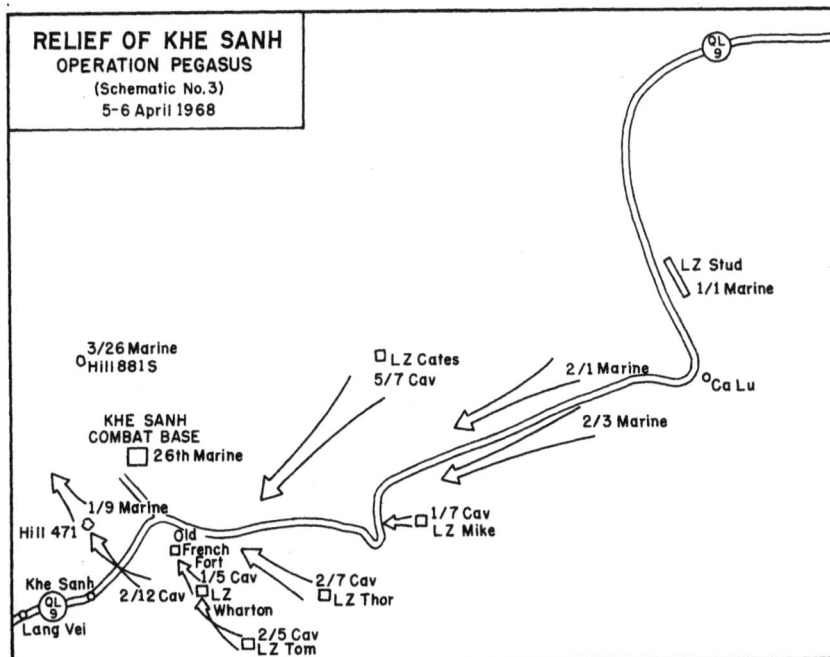

RELIEF OF KHE SANH
OPERATION PEGASUS
(Schematic No.3)
5-6 April 1968

LZ Stud
1/1 Marine

3/26 Marine
Hill 881 S

LZ Cates
5/7 Cav

2/1 Marine

Ca Lu

2/3 Marine

KHE SANH
COMBAT BASE
26th Marine

1/9 Marine

Hill 471

1/7 Cav
LZ Mike

Old
French
Fort
1/5 Cav

Khe Sanh

2/12 Cav LZ
Wharton

2/7 Cav
LZ Thor

Lang Vei

2/5 Cav
LZ Tom

MAP 13

accomplished as the 3d Brigade airlifted its command post into the base and assumed the mission of securing the position. The 2d Battalion, 7th Cavalry, cleared Route 9 to the base and linked up with the marines.

By this time it was apparent that the enemy had chosen to flee rather than face the highly mobile Americans. Vast amounts of new equipment were abandoned in place by the North Vietnamese as they hastily retreated.

Nevertheless, the enemy maintained some order in his withdrawal. At 0350 on 8 April, an element of the Vietnamese Army Airborne Task Force near the command post of the 3d Vietnamese Airborne Battalion was attacked. For over four hours the clash continued before the enemy withdrew leaving almost 75 dead behind. Later that afternoon, the 3d, 6th, and 8th Vietnamese Army Airborne Task Force closed in at Landing Zone SNAKE and began operations along Route 9 to the west.

The final battle of the operation took place on Easter Sunday, 14 April. The location was ironically between Hills 881 S and 881 N where the battle for Khe Sanh had started on 20 January. The 3d Battalion, 26th Marines, attacked from Hill 881 S to seize Hill 881 N and met heavy resistance. The marines prevailed, and the enemy withdrew leaving over 100 dead behind. (*Map 14*)

On 10 April, General Rosson had visited General Tolson, the

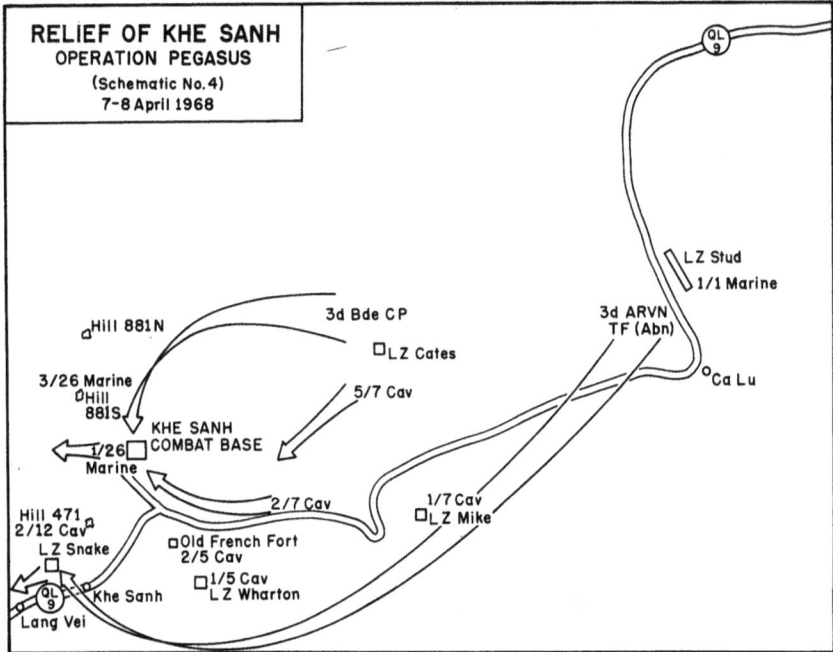

RELIEF OF KHE SANH
OPERATION PEGASUS
(Schematic No.4)
7-8 April 1968

MAP 14

commanding general of the 1st Cavalry Division, and told him to begin extracting units from PEGASUS to continue preparations for the assault into the A Shau Valley. The weather in the valley was ideal for airmobile operations at the time, and General Rosson was anxious to get the new action underway before the end of the month.

The next day, 11 April, Route 9 was officially declared open at 1600. The engineers had rebuilt 14 kilometers of road, replaced 9 key bridges, and constructed 17 by-passes. General Westmoreland described their achievement as herculean.

At 0800, on April 15, Operation PEGASUS and Operation LAM SON 207A were officially ended. The 2d Brigade came under the operational control of the 3d Marine Division, joined Task Force GLICK, and initiated Operation SCOTLAND II in the vicinity of Khe Sanh. The Vietnamese Army Airborne Task Force relocated to Hue.

The rapid and successful conclusion of Operation PEGASUS can be laid first to detailed planning and preparation. Second, the enemy was either unable to, or did not know how to, react against airmobile maneuvering of large numbers of combat troops and supporting artillery around and behind enemy positions. Third, an unprecedented degree of bomber and fighter air support was provided to the ground forces, and this combat power punched the enemy along the front line and throughout positions to his rear. Over 100,000 tons of bombs and 150,000 rounds of artillery were expended during the operation. More important, this ordnance was expended in response to excellent intelligence. Fourth, the ability to keep Khe Sanh and the troops in the field supplied was considerable. Fifth, of extreme significance was the determination and courage of the individual fighting man in the ranks.

Back to A Shau

Operation PEGASUS and the relief of Khe Sanh had been planned with an eye toward continuing the momentum of selected maneuver elements in a reconnaissance in force into the A Shau Valley. By 12 April the Provisional Corps, Vietnam, had completed a plan calling for the 1st Cavalry Division in co-operation with the 1st Vietnamese Army Division to conduct an airmobile offensive into the valley on 17 April.

During a visit to the headquarters of the Provisional Corps on 14 April, General Westmoreland chose from a hat the name DELAWARE for the operation. The plan for the operation was presented to General Westmoreland, and, while he reaffirmed his desire to go ahead with it, he disapproved the scheduled draw-down of all major units of the 1st Cavalry Division in the Khe Sanh area. General Tolson, Commanding General of the 1st Cavalry Division, General Troung, Commanding General of the 1st Vietnamese Army Division, and Major General Olinto M. Barsanti, Commanding General of the 101st Airborne Division, presented their plans for their divisions' role in Operation DELAWARE. General Rosson and General Cushman then developed a revised plan according to General Westmoreland's guidance. After a visit to the 1st Vietnamese Army Division, General Westmoreland returned to Phu Bai and approved the revised plan. The resulting operation plan 3–68 for Operation DELAWARE and Operation LAM SON 216 was published by the Provisional Corps on 16 April.

The 1st Squadron, 9th Cavalry of the 1st Cavalry Division, had been conducting extensive aerial reconnaissance in the DELAWARE area of operations during the final phases of PEGASUS. The 101st Airborne Division and the 1st Cavalry Division published instructions to bring their plans into line with the modified Provisional Corps plan on 15 and 17 April, respectively. Extensive B–52 strikes conducted between 14–19 April preceded the initiation of the operation to eliminate antiaircraft positions located during the reconnaissance phase. The 1st Brigade, 101st Airborne Division, began moving west on 16 April and the Vietnamese Army Airborne

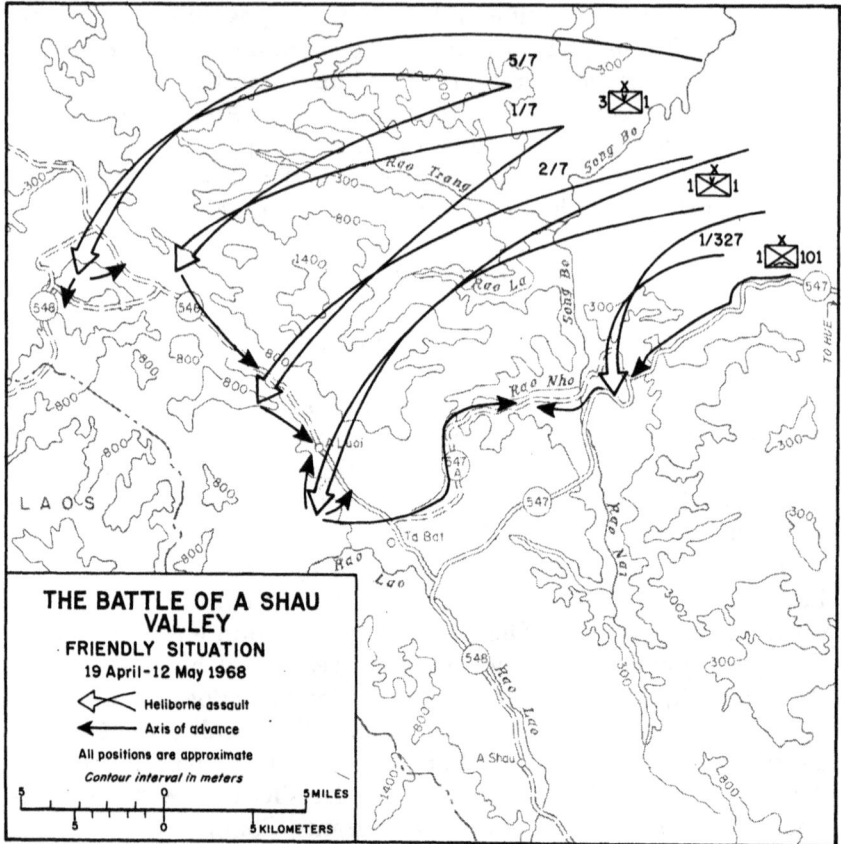

MAP 15

Task Force joined the 101st in moves to position units for the co-ordinated airmobile and ground attacks.

The operation began on the morning of 19 April. Extensive B–52 tactical air and artillery fire paved the way for the initial air assault into the A Shau Valley by the 3d Brigade, 1st Cavalry Division. Nevertheless, the antiaircraft fires that met the helicopter-borne troops were intense.

To the east, the 1st Brigade, 101st Airborne Division, began its drive westward along Route 547, shifting out of CARENTAN II into Operation DELAWARE. The 2d Battalion, 327th Infantry, attacked southwest along the road. They were followed by an air assault of the 1st Battalion, 327th Infantry, into a landing zone near the junction of Route 547 and 547 A. The next day, the 3d Brigade, 1st Cavalry Division, continued to deploy into the northern A Shau Valley as the 1st Battalion, 7th Cavalry, pushed southeast from their landing zone and the 5th Battalion, 7th Cavalry, moved to block Route 548 which entered the valley from Laos to the west. The 2d Battalion, 7th Cavalry, began an air assault to establish a landing zone further south in the valley. The 6th Vietnamese Army Airborne Battalion airlanded into the landing zone held by the 1st Battalion, 327th Infantry, and immediately made contact with the enemy upon moving out from the landing zone. (*Map 15*)

On the third day of the operation, 21 April, contact with the enemy continued as the cavalry units worked deeper into the valley. Just before noon, Company B, 1st Battalion, 7th Cavalry, discovered an enemy maintenance area which included a Soviet-manufactured bulldozer that was still operational. The 2d Battalion, 502d Infantry, air-assaulted into the area around the road junction to reinforce the 1st Battalion, 327th, and the 6th Vietnam Army Airborne Battalion.

During the initial days of the operation, the weather had been poor. Flying conditions were not as favorable as had been expected, and the helicopter assaults and Air Force cargo resupply missions were accomplished at no little risk to those involved. Conditions improved on 22 April and plans were advanced to assault the A Luoi airfield and the central portion of the valley. This insertion took place on 24 April when the 2d Battalion, 8th Cavalry, occupied a landing zone two kilometers south of the airfield. The 1st Brigade then began sweeping the surrounding area with the 1st Battalion, 12th Cavalry, to the south and east; the 2d Battalion, 8th Cavalry, to the south and west; while the 1st Battalion, 8th Cavalry, secured the landing zone.

To the south of the airfield a cache of sophisticated radio and wire communications equipment was found, indicating the advanced level of communications used by the enemy in the area. Other caches were discovered by the 1st Battalion, 7th Cavalry, to the north. Vehicles, ammunition, and three 37-mm. antiaircraft weapons were among the haul. Operation DELAWARE was spoiling the enemy's supply depots in the A Shau Valley.

During the rest of April, the buildup of friendly forces and supplies continued around the A Luoi airfield. The 3d Vietnamese Army Regimental Task Force joined the 1st Cavalry Division elements in exploiting the caches throughout the valley.

As the month of May came to A Shau, enemy resistance lessened while Operation DELAWARE units continued to find new enemy caches. By the end of the operation, the supplies denied to the enemy reached staggering proportions. On 2 May, the first cargo aircraft, a C–7A or Caribou transport landed at the A Luoi field, and on 4 May, a large C–130 landed. Aerial drop of supplies continued in order to fill supply stocks at the position.

The link-up between the cavalry forces in the valley and those moving west along Routes 547 and 547 A took place on 12 May. Company C, 1st Battalion, 12th Cavalry, represented the valley elements while the 3d Vietnamese Army Airborne Battalion was the lead unit in the westward moving forces. The meeting point was in the Rao Nho Valley some ten kilometers east-northeast of A Luoi and 25 kilometers southwest of Hue.

The extraction of the U.S. and Vietnamese from the A Shau began on 10 May and Operation DELAWARE terminated 17 May. The enemy had suffered over 850 casualties and had lost huge stockpiles of supplies. Any serious attempt by the enemy to conduct major offensive operations out of the A Shau base area would now require many months of additional preparation.

General Rosson labeled Operation DELAWARE:

... one of the most audacious, skillfully executed and successful combat undertakings of the Vietnam war ... it is significant that from its inception DELAWARE was a combined effort entailing association of the 1st Cavalry Division and the 3d ARVN Regiment, 1st ARVN Division, on the one hand, and the 101st Airborne Division and the 3d ARVN Airborne Task Force on the other. The outstanding results achieved through teamwork on the part of these combined forces reflect great credit on their leadership, professionalism, and unsurpassed fighting zeal.

The A Shau Valley campaign occurred after friendly forces had been absent from that area for two years. In a way, this operation signaled an end of one phase of the conflict. It marked the loss of enemy control of a long-held fortress and also demonstrated the control which the U.S. and South Vietnamese forces were re-establishing in the wake of the enemy's *Tet* offensive.

CHAPTER VII

Analysis of North Vietnamese Goals and Failures

The goals of the North Vietnamese in South Vietnam are summarized in Ho Chi Minh's three-point battle cry: "Defend the North, Free the South, and Unite the Country." This simple cry had much patriotic and emotional appeal, particularly since the U.S. forces were described as imperialists who had replaced the French, the former rulers of Vietnam. In the determination of military strategy and tactics and the political maneuvering to attain this goal, simplicity tended to fade away.

During 1964, the first Viet Cong division-size unit was formed and committed to combat. The Hanoi high command also decided to standardize the weapons used by its forces in the south, thus simplifying battlefield supply problems and increasing firepower. This step did have one drawback in that it required the Hanoi government to send greater tonnages of ammunition south to support the automatic weapons.

The North Vietnamese by December 1964 had reached the decision to escalate their reach for control of the south to the third and final phase of Ho Chi Minh's classical theory of revolution. They shifted from guerrilla warfare to a general offensive using major field maneuver units. The formation of the Viet Cong division and introduction of North Vietnamese Army units into the south were unmistakable evidence of this shift.

It was doubtful that the South Vietnamese could contain this increasing threat without substantial assistance. Measures were taken to provide the necessary help to strengthen the government and assist the Armed Forces. Limited numbers of U.S. Marine and U.S. Army airborne troops were deployed to South Vietnam in March 1965 to provide this assistance. Starting in July 1965, substantial numbers of U.S. Marine and Army ground forces were being deployed in South Vietnam along with required Air Force and Navy supporting forces. Thus, the pattern of enemy buildup and friendly counterbuildup was established.

The step-for-step counter to offensive enemy moves had thwarted Hanoi's aims and eventually resulted in Hanoi's apparent decision to attempt to gain their desired end through political means. In the summer of 1967, North Vietnam's Vo Nguyen Giap must have reached the decision that it would be necessary for his forces to win a significant military advantage before the start of any peace talks.

The 1968 enemy winter-spring campaign, planned in late 1967, appears to have had two major phases. In the initial phase, a series of attacks on Free World Military Assistance Forces and installations in remote areas would take place. These attacks were designed to draw major U.S. and South Vietnamese forces out of their defensive positions around the principal cities. The double-edged second phase was to consist, first, of a major attack on South Vietnam's larger cities in the expectation that the liberators would receive much popular support and, second, of a major attack directed eastward from Laos along Route 9 to capture or destroy all friendly positions from the Laotian border east to the sea.

This was a major change in enemy strategy. It was a result of the enemy's desire to repeat his 1954 success at Dien Bien Phu. As mentioned earlier, it was an admission or realization that time, once an ally, was no longer on his side.

A reassessment of the situation, made by the highest level of the Hanoi government, seemed to cause a significant redirection of goals. The enemy leadership both in Hanoi and South Vietnam took a hard critical look at how things were going in the fall of 1967. North Vietnamese combat operations had been largely unsuccessful. Despite his best efforts, his strength was declining, and his control of the population in South Vietnam was decreasing. Approximately 40 percent of the population was under North Vietnamese Army control in 1965, but this proportion had fallen to between 15 and 20 percent by September of 1967. Loss of population control meant a loss in manpower, revenues, and supplies. The North Vietnamese and Viet Cong would have to make up this deficit through greater demands on the people still under their control. Such demands would not further endear the North Vietnamese Army to the people. The relationship was already strained by the subjection of the population to more frequent military and psychological pressures by the Free World Military Assistance Forces.

The North Vietnamese Army troops had seen enough of the big picture to realize they were having little success. As a result, morale was declining drastically. Rather than generating the desired feeling of accomplishment among its troops, the Hanoi government's war-of-attrition policy was fostering a sense of despair. As the need for a North Vietnamese Army success to discredit the government of South Vietnam increased, the prospect of gaining such success had decreased.

During 1966, the North Vietnamese Army suffered approximately 93,000 killed. An estimated 35 percent of this figure comprises men who died of wounds or were permanently disabled as a result of combat actions. In 1967, the casualty figure climbed to over 145,000. During 1966 and 1967, the enemy had a total of 238,000 personnel losses. At the end of 1967, his duty strength was estimated between 210,000 and 235,000. Comparison of losses to present-for-duty strength at the beginning of 1968 indicated a personnel problem of staggering proportions.

It seemed obvious that continuation of the old war-of-attrition strategy could not possibly lead to success. After consideration of these adverse trends, the enemy adopted a new goal with these objectives: to win the war by a political and psychological campaign and to gain and maintain control of the people.

The North Vietnamese most probably chose to seek their hoped-for military victory, which they felt must precede peace talks, in the Khe Sanh area for a number of reasons. Since the target area was just across the demilitarized zone, in close proximity to good staging areas in Laos, the enemy could build up military strength and concentrate his forces outside the boundaries of South Vietnam. The remoteness of the area would complicate U.S. and Vietnamese Army resupply and support problems while at the same time favoring the North Vietnamese Army logistical situation. Also, the reaction forces coming to the aid of the attacked position would be exposed to ambush and destruction at numerous locations between Hue, Da Nang, and Khe Sanh. Once drawn into the fight, these reaction forces would be far removed from the cities which the North Vietnamese planned to attack. As noted earlier, the section of Route 1 between Quang Tri City and Hue had been a constant thorn in the flesh of the French Army during its prosecution of the Indochina War, and it was from this stretch of road that Bernard Fall drew the title of his book, *Street Without Joy*. Finally, another reason for choosing the Khe Sanh region was that this area was historically an influential Communist stronghold.

To perform the military operation, the enemy had brought four divisions plus support troops into the vicinity of Khe Sanh. In the area north of Hill 881 N, the enemy had deployed the 325C North Vietnamese Army division. Southwest of Khe Sanh was the 304th North Vietnamese Army Division and in the demilitarized zone area north of the Rock Pile was the 320th North Vietnamese Army Division. The fourth division was across the Laotian border to the west. Also around Khe Sanh were an estimated one to three armored battalions, possibly from the 203d Armored Regiment; the 68th Artillery Regiment; and elements of the 164th Artillery Regiment. Intelligence reports had further indicated the presence of at least 27 PT–76 tanks, numerous 240-mm. rocket launchers and 122-mm. assault guns, antiaircraft weapons, and at least one communication relay site.

From the enemy point of view, his revised plan for the domination of the south should have created a significant defeat for the U.S. if Khe Sanh had gone the same way Dien Bien Phu went fourteen years before. However, the enemy had made a few serious errors in his planning. High-level enemy documents of a self-analysis nature attest to these errors. He expected massive popular uprisings as his troops entered the cities and further expected large numbers of Vietnamese Armed Forces to defect to his ranks. In both these expectations he was entirely disappointed.

Having failed in his *Tet* offensive in the spring of 1968, the enemy attempted to regain momentum by maintaining constant pressure on the urban areas through continuous interdiction of lines of communication, through the imposition of a tight economic blockade, and through the destruction of the administrative control held by the government of South Vietnam. These enemy measures were meant to cause the people to demonstrate and rebel. Enemy pre-positioned and thoroughly trained political cadres could then step in and assume leadership and control of the people.

The enemy winter-spring campaign, of which *Tet* was the high-water mark, was a "Battle of the Bulge" attempt to reverse the trends of the war and create a favorable political and psychological position that would ultimately lead to the collapse of the government of the Republic of Vietnam. As of June 1968, his military efforts to achieve this goal had been totally unsuccessful. To obtain a military victory, it remained necessary for him to trigger a general uprising culminating in a successful coup d'état. Such success was impossible unless the enemy could regain his momentum and win the support of both the population and the armed forces of South Vietnam. In June of 1968, there was nothing to indicate he could gain such support. In fact the opposite effect prevailed. The *Tet* offensive was the "Pearl Harbor" of South Vietnam, arousing and uniting the people against the Communists. This public attitude resulted in large part from the ruthlessness of the Viet Cong and enabled the Vietnamese government to mobilize its manpower on a much greater scale.

There were a number of reasons for the U.S. success in defeating North Vietnamese attempts to take over the two northern provinces of South Vietnam. These included: the acquisition and analysis of enemy intelligence; the organization of forces to counter the enemy threat; air mobility; the superior ground and air firepower possessed by the Free World Military Assistance Forces; good communications; logistical support; the improvement, modest as it was, of Vietnamese Army forces; and finally, the co-ordinated actions of the divers Free World Force elements which operated to contain and defeat the enemy.

Intelligence

Information about the enemy is an invaluable asset in any military conflict and proved itself especially so in Vietnam. In a conventional struggle, one can at least engage the enemy; that is, observe him and take him under fire, even if his immediate intentions, strength, equipment, and unit organizations are unknown. In the guerrilla environment of South Vietnam two very critical unknown factors existed. It was difficult to know *where* and *who* the enemy was. In the populated areas, much importance was placed on determining who the enemy was while in the unpopulated regions, the problem was learning where the enemy was.

The intelligence effort was increased in response to the enemy concentration of forces in and around northern I Corps. Civilian agents, military patrols, long-range reconnaissance patrols, aerial observers particularly from helicopters, the Civilian Irregular Defense Group forces at Lang Vei, Special Forces teams operating in the A Shau Valley, and radio interceptors provided a steady stream of information about the enemy's activities.

An extensive reconnaissance program in early January was initiated to obtain as much information as possible about the enemy. This effort, code-named NIAGARA I, included all sources of information, and aimed at developing target information about the enemy in northern I Corps and the adjacent area immediately to the west of the Laotian border. The information was derived from, among additional sources, aerial and ground searches, interrogation of prisoners and other persons that may have been in or passed through the area, and study of captured enemy documents.

After the enemy's *Tet* offensive in 1968, Operation LEAP FROG was instituted as an accelerated effort to obtain intelligence indicating the enemy's goals in the campaign. Such knowledge would identify his future moves, thus making possible the formulation of friendly countermoves.

Allied intelligence analysis concluded that the attacks were politically motivated and aimed at seizing the urban areas, at the replacement of Republic of Vietnam officials with members of the Viet Cong infrastructure, and possibly, after having established a position of power from which to negotiate, at suing for a coalition government.

CHART 4—BUILDUP OF OPPOSING MANEUVER BATTALIONS IN
I CORPS TACTICAL ZONE [1]

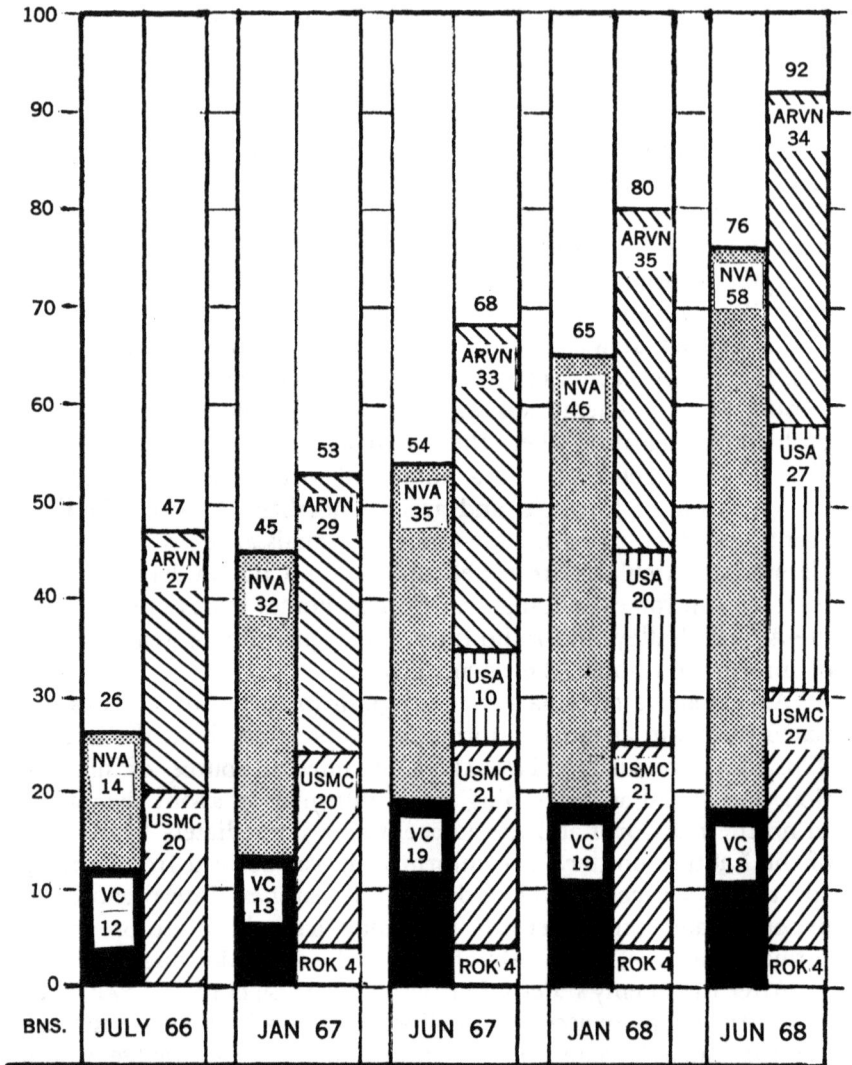

[1] This graph displays only infantry type maneuver battalions.

Organization for Combat

The responses to this intelligence were reflected in the continued gradual movement of the III Marine Amphibious Force into
the northern segment of the corps area and the influx of United

States Army and Republic of Korea Army troops in an effort to increase the density of the Free World Forces in the threatened area. The Military Assistance Command and Command Post was initially organized to control the deployment of a U.S. Army corps into the area. The organization and deployment of Task Force OREGON and the headquarters of Provisional Corps, Vietnam, have already been discussed. In May of 1968, there were 98 maneuver battalions in the corps area of which 26 were U.S. Marine Corps, 31 were U.S. Army, 37 were Vietnamese, and 4 were Republic of Korea. This total, 196, was somewhat above the June figure and is indicative of the fluid situation. (Chart 4)

The U.S. maneuver battalions were assigned to the 1st and 3d Marine Divisions, 1st Cavalry Division (Airmobile), 101st Airborne Division, and the Americal Division; the Vietnamese Army battalions were normally assigned to, or under, the operational control of the 1st and 2d Vietnamese Army Divisions and the 51st Independent Infantry Regiment. The four Republic of Korea battalions were under the 2d Republic of Korea Marine Brigade which, although not under the operational control of the III Marine Amphibious Force, was generally treated as such for planning and coordinating purposes.

The flexibility of the III Marine Amphibious Force organization was attested to by the mix of Army and Marine units under various command echelons. Both Army and Marine battalions were considered to be basically interchangeable during the preparation of operation plans. Reporting directly to the III Marine Amphibious Force were Provisional Corps, Vietnam; C Company, 5th U.S. of operation plans. Reporting directly to the III Marine Amphibious Force were Provisional Corps, Vietnam; C Company, 5th U.S. Special Forces; 1st Marine Air Wing; 1st Marine Division; 23d or Americal Division, and, informally, the 2d Republic of Korea Marine Brigade. (Chart 5)

Within Provisional Corps, Vietnam, were three divisions. The 3d Marine Division was reinforced from three to five Marine Regiments and, in May 1968, reinforced by the 2d Brigade, 1st Air Cavalry Division. The 1st Air Cavalry Division had its two organic brigades and the 196th Light Infantry Brigade. The 101st Airborne Division had two organic brigades and the 3d Brigade, 82d Airborne Division. The organization for combat of Army and Marine units was dictated by the tactical situation.

The flexibility of the U.S. forces, and their ability to shift Army, Navy, and Marine combat and combat support units among the various headquarters in response to changes in the tactical situation was a major contribution to the success of operations against the

CHART 5—SUBORDINATE UNITS TO 3D MARINE AMPHIBIOUS FORCE

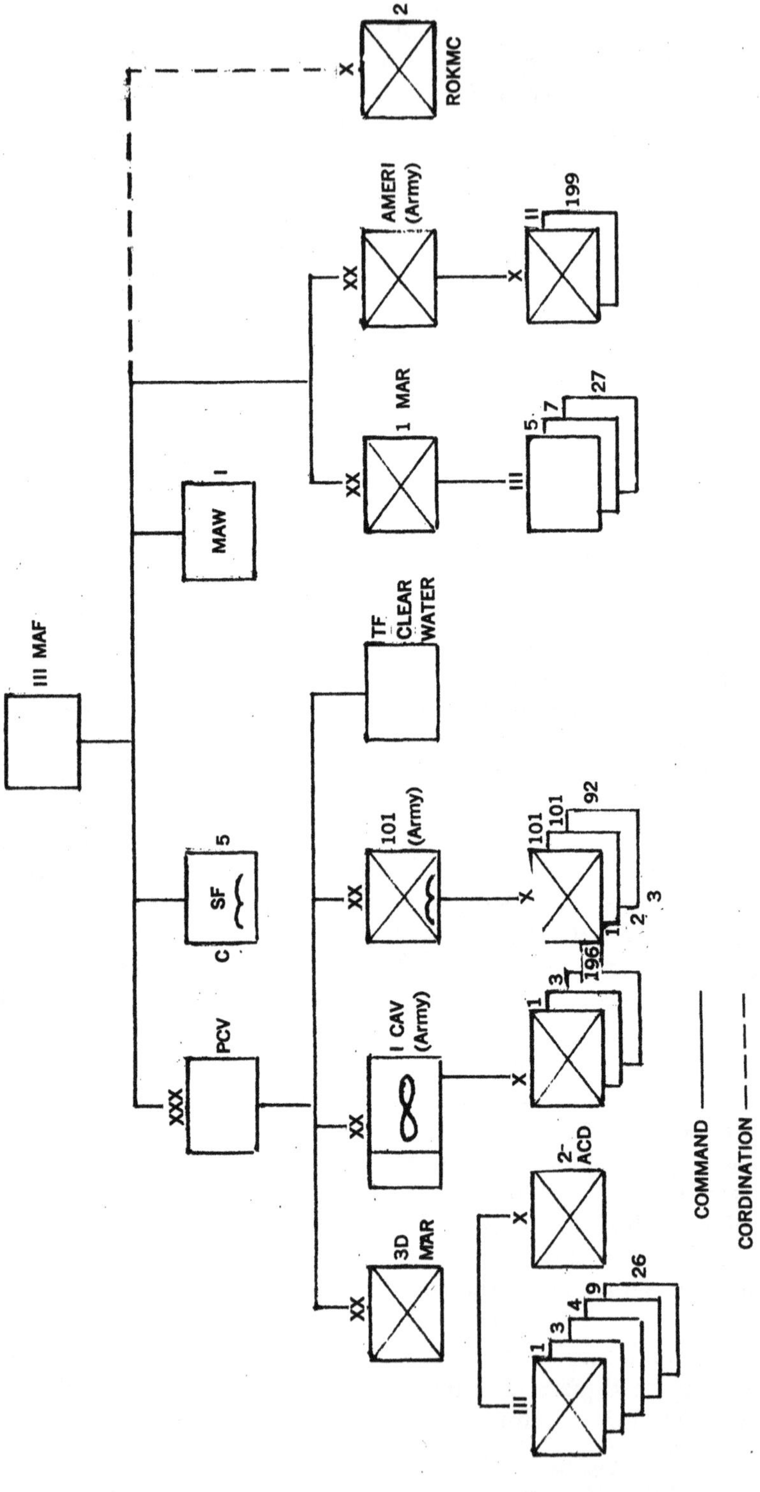

enemy in I Corps. This flexibility also facilitated the implementation of cross-servicing agreements.

Airmobility

Airmobility provided a proportionate increase in the combat potential of combat units. From a tactical point of view, the helicopter gave unit commanders a new dimension in warfare—vertical envelopment of an enemy's rear or flank. For centuries commanders have sought to outflank their enemies, by foot, by cavalry, and even by elephants—and more recently by tanks and by airborne forces. The helicopter provided this ability to U.S. forces in Vietnam on an unprecedented scale. The 85 knots per hour helicopter placed troops at decisive points in time to influence the outcome of the battle. This ability had a multiplying effect on U.S. combat power.

The helicopter was the work horse of the Vietnam War. Despite the helicopter's sensitivity to weather conditions, its versatility gave it great value in combat operations. In addition to being faster than ground vehicles, it had the important advantage of being able to disregard the ruggedness of terrain. The helicopter rescued people from minefields, plucked them from the water, captured prisoners of war, and evacuated casualties from the scene of battle to supporting hospitals, including naval hospitals afloat.

Superior Firepower

The massive firepower available to units of the Free World Military Assistance Forces dominated actions in the air, on the ground, and at sea. Artillery, aerial rocket artillery, naval gun fire, tactical fighter-bombers, and stragetic bombers brought awesome destructive power to bear on enemy units.

Following the target acquisition program under NIAGARA I the successive artillery and air firepower operation was designated NIAGARA II. The massive close air support provided under the single manager concept for air is described in the concluding pages of Chapter IV.

B–52 raids were an important factor in the program. The heavy bombing raids generated many casualties and created fear and low morale among enemy troops while bolstering morale within friendly units. The raids forced enemy units of battalion and regimental size to evacuate elaborately prepared positions, thus abandoning sites in which considerable resources had been invested.

Communications

The upswing of activity along the demilitarized zone and within the two northern provinces demanded a vast and rapid increase in teletype and voice communications channels to handle expansion of operational and logistical traffic. The influx of additional Marine units, two Army divisions, plus associated combat service support and combat support units, and the eventual organization of the Military Assistance Forward Command Post succeeded by the Provisional Corps, Vietnam, added to the need for expanded communications.

Within a 30-day period, U.S. Army, Vietnam, organized the 63d Signal Battalion, 1st Signal Brigade of the Strategic Communications Command, concurrently with the organization of the Military Assistance Forward Command Post and the Provisional Corps, Vietnam. During that short time frame the unit grew from a headquarters nucleus in Phu Bai to a 1300-man, three company battalion. With tactical and mobile contingency equipment flown in from various areas in Vietnam and Thailand, the battalion established command control and area communications for Military Assistance Command Post Forward, Provisional Corps, and the III Marine Amphibious Force. At the same time, U.S. Air Force elements provided a 60-channel system from Dong Ha to Phu Bai and thence to Da Nang, furnishing the needed communications gateway to the commanders of the U.S. Military Assistance Command and the U.S. Army, Vietnam, through the Defense Communications System.

During Operations PEGASUS and DELAWARE, when the tactical command posts of the 101st Airborne and 1st Cavalry Divisions moved into the Ca Lu and A Shau area, mobile 12- and 24-channel very high frequency radio relay and tropospheric scatter systems were extended to these field locations from Phu Bai.

Logistics

Moving large troop units into the undeveloped northern region required prodigious effort in construction of logistical facilities and in operational planning down to the finest details. Maneuvering of combat troops placed enormous strain on the transportation capabilities, and resupplying the troops in new distant locations was a formidable task.

Logistical planning kept pace with the buildup of U.S. forces in I Corps. Procedures were developed by the U.S. Navy for the initial support to Army units deployed north. As the Military Assistance Forward Command Post and the equivalent of a U.S. army corps deployed to the 1st Corps Tactical Zone, a forward area support base was organized at Da Nang to support them and handle the heavy volume of supplies.

Transportation was improved as Highway 1 reopened and the fuel pipeline was restored. A logistical-over-the-shore (LOTS) facility was constructed, and a new pipeline laid from the LOTS facility into Dong Ha. Finally the Phu Bai airport had been expanded to increase its tonnage handling.

In general, resupply was accomplished by surface means to the maximum extent possible. However, some operations required aerial supply for certain elements of a unit or even for the entire unit. This need prevailed at the garrison at Khe Sanh. The calculation of aerial resupply capabilities was for this reason an important step in planning.

The advantage of surprise in military operations could easily be lost if impending actions were revealed by pre-stocking supplies in a new operational area. It was therefore necessary to move vast amounts of supplies into a new area at the same time the combat troops moved in. This generated major fluctuations in requirements for aircraft and trucks during the deployment period.

In allocating resources available to conduct resupply during an upcoming operation, there were many opportunities to substitute one resource for another. Operation PEGASUS was an example of this fact. The Khe Sanh garrison was entirely supplied by cargo aircraft, its outposts by helicopter. The closing relief forces were supplied by air or truck convoy, depending upon their proximity to Route 9 and the engineers' progress in rebuilding the route. Although there is little resemblance between a C–130 cargo aircraft, a CH–47 helicopter, and the engineer bulldozer–supply truck combination, from a logistical standpoint, they accomplished the same thing. It was a matter of selecting the most economical means or simply using what was available.

Improvement of Vietnamese Armed Forces

While units of the Free World Military Assistance Forces shouldered the burden of containing the enemy offensives, modest gains were made in improving the combat capability of Republic of Vietnam military forces. This feat was accomplished by providing military advisers to help Vietnamese commanders solve the complexities of tactical and logistical problems. Changes were made in the military school system to more adequately address contemporary problems. (*Chart 6*)

Another step was to revamp the promotion system for better

CHART 6—I CORPS VIETNAMESE ORGANIZATION

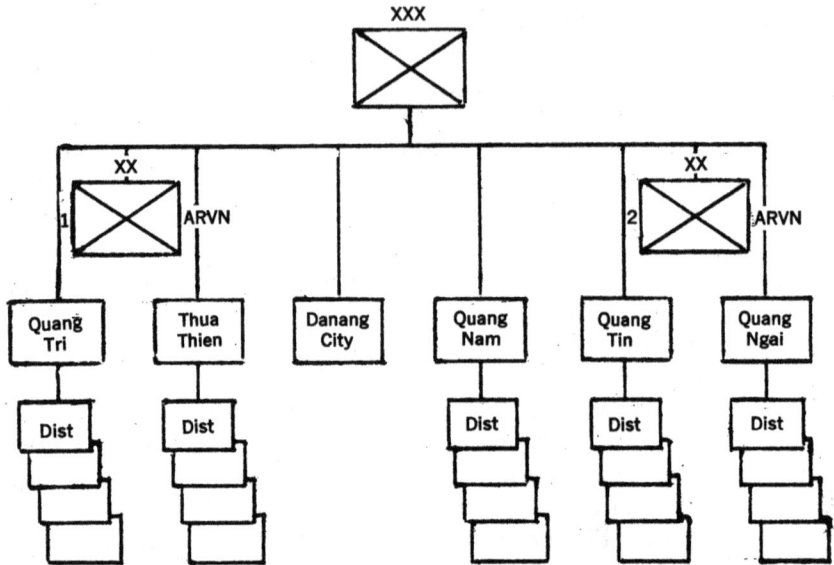

DIVISIONS, PROVINCES, AND DISTRICTS

recognition of the merit of officers and noncommissioned officers. The senior Vietnamese officers began to summarily relieve incompetents, reprimand weakness in subordinate's leadership, and give recognition to superior performance. One statistical measure of the general improvement of the military forces was the decreasing desertion rate. Another measure, and a significant one, was the growing number of Vietnamese units that earned the United States Presidential Unit Citation for their heroic actions in combat. During and following the 1968 *Tet* offensive, the military forces of South Vietnam acquitted themselves adequately. In many cases, such as that of the 1st Vietnamese Division in Hue, they fought with distinction.

Along with the qualitative betterment of personnel, strides were taken in improving the equipment of the armed forces. Vietnamization began with the issue of the M16 rifle, mainstay weapon of U.S. ground services, to Vietnamese Army units. Better machine guns, mortars, and other crew-served weapons were added to the Vietnamese Army inventory. In addition to these weapons, the issue of aircraft, boats, helicopters, tanks, and armored personnel carriers improved the ability of the Vietnamese to reposition their forces as required by changes in the tactical situation. The morale of the Vietnamese rose greatly upon receipt of this modern equipment.

Each Saturday morning, the commanding general of the III Marine Amphibious Force was briefed on Vietnamese Army operations by the U.S. advisers to I Corps. Following the briefing, a commander's conference was held at the headquarters of General Hoang Xuan Lam to discuss matters of mutual concern. The agenda, usually distributed in advance, covered planned operations, both unilateral and combined, which required co-ordination and co-operation of Free World Military Assistance support. The extensive exchange of liaison officers down to battalion level, when required, was a common practice throughout I Corps.

The U.S. commanders worked closely with the Vietnamese commanders adjacent to their areas of responsibility and provided excellent support on a routine basis. The co-operation was extended to other Free World Military commanders as in the case of Brigadier General Kim Yun Sang of the 2d Republic of Korea Marine Brigade.

By 1968, combined operations were becoming the rule rather than the exception. Operations PEGASUS and DELAWARE were prime examples of such operations conducted in I Corps during the first four months of 1968.

Co-operation between Vietnamese Army and Free World Military Assistance Forces also extended to logistics and training. Vietnamese Army elements operating with U.S. units received logistical support from those units. On the training side, two examples serve to demonstrate the mutual benefit derived from this practice. In 1967, the 3d Battalion, 6th Vietnamese Regiment, trained companies of the newly arrived 198th U.S. Infantry Brigade in Viet Cong tactics, the detection of mines and booby traps, and the techniques of Viet Cong village search. That same year, the 3d Marine Division trained 2,430 men of the 2d Vietnamese Army Regiment in use of the M16 rifle.

Co-ordination of artillery fires and air strikes with one another were also accomplished by Vietnamese, U.S., and Free World Military Assistance Forces throughout I Corps. This co-ordination was done at the division level in both the 1st and 2d Vietnamese Division areas, and included U.S. naval gun fire.

The Other War

The failure of the North Vietnamese to gain control of the population of South Vietnam was not an outcome of unsuccessful combat actions alone. Also contributing to their failure was the fact that the South Vietnamese government developed many programs supporting the economic, social, and political goals of the population. To obtain popular support, the government announced these new programs after the 8 February 1966 Honolulu Conference. The government pronouncement called on all citizens of South Vietnam to work together to develop the country:

We must bring about a true social revolution and construct a modern society in which every man can know that he has a future . . . To those future citizens of a free, democratic South Vietnam now fighting with the Viet Cong, we take this occasion to say come and join in this national revolutionary adventure:
—come safely to join us through the Open Arms Programs,
—stop killing your brothers, sisters, their elders, and their children,
—come and work through constitutional democracy to build together that life of dignity, freedom, and peace those in the North would deny the people of Vietnam.

Along with implementation of a new constitution, the government established the revolutionary development program to initiate the social, economic, and political reforms needed to improve the life of the rural population, and to strengthen their confidence in the government and its resistance to the Viet Cong. The program sent teams of 59 men, armed for self-defense, into recently secured areas to help establish local security, weed out any remaining Viet Cong, and initiate a development program.

Two additional actions that had good results were the *Chieu Hoi* or Open Arms Progran and the *Doan Ket* or National Reconciliation Program. The former program began as early as 1963 when more than 5,700 Viet Cong accepted the opportunity to return to the government during the initial four months of the declared amnesty period. As additional combat troops took the field against the enemy, the number of enemy soldiers rallying to the government increased.

When a man returned to the government under this program, he was interviewed to determine his sincerity, rewarded for any weapons or equipment turned in, and placed in a re-education program through which he learned the aims and purposes of the government of South Vietnam and the role of the Free World Military Assistance Forces in the war. An added bonus in this program was the fact that an estimated 30 percent of the returnees then served in the government armed forces.

The second program, *Doan Ket*, offered more to the middle and upper ranks of the enemy hierarchy than the *Chieu Hoi* amnesty program. This program included provisions that returnees would be employed in accordance with their ability, presumably in positions at a level comparable to those they had in the enemy system. This added a bit to the motivation of senior persons who might be inclined to terminate their relationship with the enemy. This program also included a re-educational process before personnel were declared graduates and returned to full citizenship status.

Conclusion

The North Vietnamese failed to achieve victory in the northern provinces in 1968 because their efforts to gain and retain control of the population and the government of South Vietnam were obstructed by determined U.S. and Free World Military Assistance Forces. During the critical period when the enemy upgraded his operations from insurgency and guerrilla actions to a full-scale conventional invasion, enemy aims were thwarted by military action. The success of the Free World Forces can be attributed to their flexibility in organization and tactics to meet the ever changing enemy situation and their mutual co-operation in conducting combined operations against the foe. The success was also due to the steady improvement of the South Vietnamese Armed Forces—a long-term goal of the headquarters of the Military Assistance Command, Vietnam. The establishment of programs to win the allegiance of the people to their government by eliminating the social, political, and economic injustices which provided a fertile environment for insurgency also furthered success.

A final tribute must be paid to the fighting heart of the individual soldier, sailor, marine, airman, and civilian who faced the dangers of a cruel enemy. Although scientists have invented weapons that have revolutionized warfare, they have not been able to replace the soldier on the ground. He was aggressive, physically fit, eager to fight, with pride in his profession and compassion for the Vietnamese people—a superb fighter in the finest traditions of great Americans, great patriots, and great soldiers.

Glossary

ABN	Airborne
ACD	1st Air Cavalry Division
ADC	Assistant division commander
AMERI	Americal Division
AMMO	Ammunation
ARTY	Artillery
ARVN	Army, Republic of Vietnam
AT	Antitank
BARC	Barge, Amphibious Resupply Cargo
BDE	Brigade
Bladder boat	Inflatable non-self-propelled watercraft
BN	Battalion
B40/41	Grenade propelled by rocket
C.A.	Combined Action
CAV	Cavalry
CIDG	Civilian Irregular Defense Group (Vietnamese)
CH–47	Cargo helicopter
CO	Company
CP	Command post
CRP	Corps
CTZ	Corps tactical zone
C–7A or Caribou	Small cargo aircraft
C–123	Medium cargo aircraft
C–130	Large cargo aircraft
DMZ	Demilitarized zone
FFV	Field Force, Vietnam
Flareship	Aircraft configured to drop illumination flares
FSB	Fire support base
FWMAF	Free World Military Assistance Forces
HOW	Howitzer
HQ	Headquarters
LARC	Lighter, amphibious, resupply cargo
LAW	Light anti-tank weapon

LCU	Landing craft, utility
LCM	Landing craft, mechanized
LOTS	Logistical-over-the-shore
LST	Landing ship, tank
LZ	Landing zone
MACV	Military Assistance Command, Vietnam
MACV FWD	Military Assistance Command, Vietnam, Forward Command Post
III MAF	III Marine Amphibious Force
MAR	Marine
MAW	Marine Air Wing
M16	Rapid firing light automatic rifle
NVA	North Vietnamese Army
Ontos	6-Tubed 106-mm. recoilless rifle
PBR	Patrol boat, river
PCV	Provisional Corps, Vietnam
POL	Petroleum, oil, lubricants
PROV	Provisional
PT–76	Russian manufactured light amphibious tank
QUAD–50	4 barrelled 50-Caliber air defense machine gun
Readout	A device that displays in digits data computed or registered
RECON	Reconnaissance
ROK	Republic of Korea
RPG	Rocket propelled grenade
RR	Recoilless rifle
Seabees	Navy construction battalion
SF	Special Forces
Signal Hill	High terrain upon which communication antennas are mounted
SVN	South Vietnam
Tet	Lunar new year
TF	Task Force
TOC	Tactical operations center
UH–1H	Utility helicopter
USA	United States Army

USAF	United States Air Force
USARV	United States Army, Vietnam
USMC	United States Marine Corps
USN	United States Navy
VC	Viet Cong
VN	Vietnamese
VNN	Vietnamese Navy
X-RAY	A Marine task force in 1968

Index

A Luoi airfield: 91
A Shau: 3, 6–7, 28, 30, 69–70, 78–79, 88–92, 97, 102
Abrams, General Creighton W.: 45, 47, 59, 63, 66–69
Acoustic sensors: 21
Advisers, military: 103, 105
Air operations: 6, 18, 60, 71–72, 74–77, 80–81, 83–85, 88, 90–91, 101
Airborne Regiment, 501st: 45
Aircraft. *See also* Helicopters.
  B–52: 31, 72, 90, 101
  C–7A: 91
  C–123: 83
  C–130: 15, 75–76, 83, 91
  electronic warfare: 31
Airfields: 8, 15, 26, 91
Airmobile Divisions
  1st Cavalry: 35, 43–44, 47–49, 53, 55–57, 67, 70, 78–81, 84–85, 87, 89–92, 99, 102
  82d Airborne: 68, 99
  101st Airborne: 45, 55, 66, 70, 78, 81, 89–90, 92, 99, 102
  502d Airborne: 81
Americal Division: 99
Amphibious resupply cargo barges (BARC's): 60
Amphibious resupply cargo lighters (LARC's): 60
Annamite Mountains: 3, 16
Anti-infiltration system: 21–24
Armor Regiment, 34th: 81
Artillery piece, 152-mm.: 18
Artillery Regiments
  21st: 85
  77th: 85
Australian advisers: 24

Ban Me Thuot: 37, 39
Barsanti, Major General Olinto M.: 89
Ben Hai River: 16
Ben Tre: 37, 39
Brewer, Robert: 55, 57

Buddhists: 4, 8
Bunker, Ellsworth: 37

Ca Lu: 70, 81, 84, 102
Cam Lo: 9
Cam Ranh Bay: 26
Camp Carroll: 13, 15, 32
Camp Evans: 45, 78
Can Tho: 37, 39
Caruthers, Brigadier General Lawrence H.: 69
Casualties: 48, 75, 95
Cavalry Regiments
  1st Air: 45–46
  5th: 55–56, 81, 84–86
  7th: 44–46, 83, 85, 87, 90–91
  8th: 55, 91
  9th: 14
  11th Armored: 14
  12th: 44–45, 55–56, 85–86, 91–92
Chemical smoke generator companies: 5
Chu Lai: 6, 14–15, 26
Citadel: 39–47, 68
Co Roc Mountains: 76
Combat service support elements: 5, 14
Communications: 15, 41, 66–67, 70–71, 91, 96, 102
Con Thien: 13, 16, 18, 69, 79
Congressional hearings: 22
Convoy Control Center: 59
Convoys, river: 64–65
Corps tactical zones
  I: 4, 6, 8–9, 11–12, 15, 21–22, 24–26, 28–31, 35–37, 40, 45, 50, 57–59, 62, 66–68, 71–72, 78–79, 97, 101, 103, 105
  II: 15, 37
  III: 15
Crachin: 4
Cua Viet River: 58, 63–65
Cushman, Lieutenant General Robert E.: 34, 45, 67–69, 74, 79, 89

Da Nang: 4, 6, 8, 11, 26–29, 37, 45, 59, 69–70, 79, 95, 102–03

Low Altitude Parachute Extraction System (LAPES): 76
Lownds, Colonel David E.: 31–32, 77

Machine gun, M60: 28
MaNamara Line: 21
Matheson, Brigadier General Salve H.: 66
Military police support: 14
Momyer, General William W., USAF: 71
Monsoons: 3–4, 40
Mortars, 60-mm.: 28
Mortars, 82-mm.: 33
Mortars, 120-mm.: 8
Munster, Colonel Daniel F.: 58–59
My Tho: 37

National Reconciliation Program: 106
Naval gunfire: 43, 46, 101, 105
Navy Support Activity, Da Nang: 70
Nha Trang: 37, 71
North Vietnamese Army: 5–6, 18–19, 32–34, 37, 40, 48, 94
  2d Division: 30
  5th Division: 30
  304th Division: 29-30, 49, 77, 85, 95
  308th Division: 30
  320th Division: 29, 95
  324B Division: 9, 11, 29–30, 49
  325C Division: 17–18, 29–30, 49, 95
  341st Division: 30
  4th Regiment: 41–42
  6th Regiment: 41, 49
  68th Armored Regiment: 30, 95
  95B Regiment: 6
  101C Regiment: 6
  164th Artillery Regiment: 30, 95
  203d Armored Regiment: 95
  812th Regiment: 51
  K4B Battalion: 42–43, 51, 53
  K–5 Battalion: 53
  K–6 Battalion: 53, 56
  K–8 Battalion: 53
  10th Sapper Battalion: 51
  12th Sapper Battalion: 41–42
  800th Battalion: 41
  802d Battalion: 41
  804th Battalion: 41–42
  806th Battalion: 42
  810th Battalion: 43

Ontos: 32
Open Arms Program: 106

Operations
  DELAWARE: 89–92, 102, 105
  HASTINGS: 9
  HICKORY: 18
  LAM SON 216: 89
  LEAP FROG: 49, 97
  NIAGARA I: 31, 35, 83, 97, 101
  NIAGARA II: 31, 35, 76, 101
  PEGASUS: 70, 79, 81, 83–89, 102–03, 105
  PRAIRIE: 11
  SCOTLAND: 77, 88
  STARLIGHT: 6

Patrol boats: 63–65
Pearson, Major General Willard: 66, 69
Perfume River: 39
Petroleum, oils, and lubricants: 15, 59, 70
Phu Bai: 6, 11, 26, 35, 43, 45, 53, 58, 62, 66–69, 102–03
Phu Cam: 46
Pipe lines: 15, 26, 58–59, 103
Ports: 4, 15, 26–27
Pridgen, Colonel Robert B.: 14
Provisional Corps, Vietnam: 68–71, 79, 89, 99, 102
Provisional infantry division: 13–14

Quang Nam Province: 3–4, 26, 28
Quang Ngai Province: 26, 28, 50
Quang Tri: 4, 16, 35, 37, 45, 50–51, 53, 56–59, 69, 95
Quang Tri Province: 3–4, 9, 11, 28, 34, 49, 57, 66, 78
Qui Nhon: 37

Rao Nho Valley: 92
Rattan, Colonel Donald V.: 53, 55
Report on the War in Vietnam: 34
Republic of Korea: 25
Republic of Korea Army: 99
Republic of Korea 2d (Dragon) Marine Brigade: 24, 26, 99, 105
Republic of Vietnam Air Force: 6
Republic of Vietnam Army: 6, 10, 21–22, 48, 55, 97, 103–05, 107
  1st Division: 9, 28, 40, 43, 45–47, 50, 69, 79, 81, 89, 92, 99
  2d Division: 28, 50, 99
  1st Infantry Regiment: 81
  1st Regiment: 51, 53, 55
  2d Infantry Regiment: 81, 105
  6th Regiment: 105

www.ingramcontent.com/pod-product-compliance
Lightning Source LLC
Chambersburg PA
CBHW052114090426
42741CB00009B/1809